DOURO RIVE

TRAVEL GUIDE 2024

Expert Guide for First Time Visitor To The Best Historical Landmarks, Hidden Gems, Top Destinations and is Packed With Helpful Recommendations and Packing Tips

GLOBAL
DESTINATIONS
CARAWAY TRAVELS

Richard Caraway

Disclaimer

The information contained in this travel guide is, to the best of the author's knowledge, accurate and up-to-date at the time of publication. However, the author and publisher make no guarantees, expressed or implied, about the completeness, reliability, or suitability of the information provided.

This guide is intended to be used for informational purposes only and should not be relied upon as a sole source of information when planning a trip to the Duoro River region. The author and publisher strongly recommend that travellers conduct additional research, consult local resources, and exercise their own judgment and caution when making travel arrangements and decisions.

The author and publisher shall not be held liable for any loss, injury, or damage incurred by the reader, either directly or indirectly, as a consequence of using the information provided in this travel guide. Travellers are responsible for their own safety and well-being while exploring the Duoro River region.

Contents

CHAPTER 1.

INTRODUCTION

About the Douro River

As an experienced Douro River cruise guide, I can say with certainty that the Douro is one of the most captivating and picturesque waterways in all of Europe. Flowing for over 550 miles through Spain and Portugal, the Douro carves a dramatic path through the heart of the Iberian Peninsula, winding its way past steep, terraced vineyards, quaint riverside villages, and historic port cities.

The Douro's origins can be traced back thousands of years to the ancient Iberian civilizations that first settled along its banks. The river played a vital role in the development of the region, serving as a crucial trade route and the lifeblood for the production of

Portugal's renowned port wine. Even today, the Douro remains inextricably linked to the cultural heritage and traditions of the Douro Valley.

What truly sets the Douro apart, however, is its stunning natural beauty. As the river flows westward towards the Atlantic Ocean, it is flanked by towering schist cliffs and rolling hills blanketed in vibrant green vineyards. The landscape is so dramatically sculpted that UNESCO has designated the Douro Valley as a World Heritage site, recognizing it as an outstanding example of a traditional wine-producing region.

For the traveler, a cruise along the Douro offers a one-of-a-kind opportunity to immerse oneself in the history, culture, and breathtaking scenery of this remarkable corner of the Iberian Peninsula. Whether you're sipping port at a family-owned quinta, hiking through terraced vineyards, or simply admiring the views from the deck of your river cruise ship, the Douro has a way of captivating all who experience its charms.

As you plan your own Douro River adventure, I encourage you to enjoy the river's leisurely pace and allow yourself to be swept away by its timeless allure. From the UNESCO-listed medieval city of Porto to the remote, vine-draped hillsides of the Douro Valley, this is a place that will leave a lasting impression on your heart and mind. Pack your bags, board the Douro, and embark on an unforgettable journey through one of Europe's most enchanting regions.

History and Culture of the Douro Valley

The Douro Valley is a region steeped in a rich, centuries-old history and culture that has become inextricably entwined with the meandering course of the River Douro. This enchanting corner of Portugal has long captivated travellers and scholars alike, offering a compelling glimpse into the Iberian Peninsula's storied past.

The Douro Valley's history dates back thousands of years, when ancient Iberian tribes first settled the region. Pre-Roman civilisations were drawn to the Douro's fertile banks and natural bounty, as evidenced by artifacts and archaeological sites throughout the valley. However, it was the Romans who truly established the Douro Valley's lasting legacy. In the first century AD, the Romans established settlements along the river and began growing grapes for wine production, a practice that would define the region for centuries to come.

During the medieval period, the Douro Valley was under Moorish rule before being reconquered by Christian kingdoms in the 12th century. During this time, merchants in the coastal city of Porto began shipping the region's rich, fortified wines to England and elsewhere, establishing the iconic Port wine trade. The Douro Valley's reputation as a premier wine-producing area grew over the centuries, with established quintas (wine estates) and time-honored viticultural techniques becoming the region's hallmarks.

The Douro Valley's cultural heritage is most evident in its picturesque towns and villages. Porto, the valley's largest city and a UNESCO World Heritage site, is a living testament to the region's maritime heritage, with colorful medieval alleyways, grand Baroque churches, and iconic iron bridges spanning the Douro River. Historic settlements such as Régua, Pinhão, and Lamego highlight the valley's viticulture heritage, with tile-roofed houses and town squares surrounded by terraced vineyards and centuries-old wine cellars.

However, the Douro Valley's cultural riches extend beyond its architectural wonders and oenological traditions. The region is also known for its vibrant folklore, music, and artisanal crafts.

Traditional folk dances, such as the energetic vira and the stately pauliteiros, continue to be performed at local festivals, while the melancholic sounds of the Portuguese guitar and the powerful, soulful fado music reverberate throughout the valley. Visitors can also find a variety of handcrafted ceramics, embroidered textiles, and intricate filigree jewelry, all reflecting the Douro's rich artisanal heritage.

The Douro Valley's remarkable natural environment serves as the foundation for this rich cultural tapestry, shaping the region's identity. The dramatic, terraced vineyards that cascade down the valley's steep, schist-lined slopes are more than just a scenic backdrop; they also demonstrate the ingenuity and resilience of the Douro's wine growers, who have tailored their viticulture practices to the region's rugged terrain. Meanwhile, the river has long served as the valley's lifeblood, allowing for trade, transportation, and the growth of riverside communities.

Today, as the Douro Valley faces modernization and globalization challenges, its people remain steadfast in their commitment to preserving the region's time-honored traditions and cultural identity. From the family-run quintas that continue to produce world-class Port and table wines to the local artisans who uphold centuries-old craft techniques, the Douro Valley exemplifies how a region can embrace progress while honoring its past. This delicate balance, this seamless blend of history and modernity, is what makes the Douro Valley such an appealing and enriching destination for travelers looking to immerse themselves in Portugal's authentic heart.

Why a Douro River Cruise is a Must-Do Experience and why it Should Be in Your Travel Bucket List.

For the discerning traveller seeking an unparalleled journey through one of Europe's most remarkable regions, a Douro River cruise stands out as a must-do experience that should undoubtedly be at the top of your travel bucket list. Meandering through the UNESCO-protected Douro Valley, these enchanting voyages offer an immersive and utterly captivating window into the history, culture, and breathtaking natural beauty of Portugal's premier wine-producing heartland.

A Douro River cruise is truly unique in that it allows you to see the valley's ever-changing landscape up close and at your leisure. As your luxury river ship glides along the gentle currents, you'll be treated to an ever-changing panorama of terraced vineyards, historic quintas, picturesque riverside towns, and dramatic, sheer-sided hills - a cinematic experience that no other mode of transportation can provide. This leisurely pace allows you to fully appreciate the tranquil atmosphere of the Douro, savour the scent of ripening grapes, and connect with the rhythms of daily life along the riverbanks.

However, a Douro River cruise provides much more than just a scenic float through the countryside. These voyages also offer an unparalleled opportunity to delve into the region's rich cultural tapestry, with shore excursions that give you exclusive access to historic wine estates, charming towns, and UNESCO-listed architectural gems. Explore Porto's medieval streets, admire its iconic bridges and baroque buildings, learn about Port wine production at a family-owned quinta, or visit Pinhão, a picturesque town with a tiled train station and panoramic views of vineyard-clad hills. These immersive experiences not only enlighten and educate, but they also create a lasting bond between the traveller and the Douro Valley's vibrant cultural heritage.

Furthermore, a Douro River cruise offers all of this while also providing world-class onboard amenities and service. Sailing aboard a cutting-edge river ship, you'll enjoy luxurious accommodations, gourmet cuisine that highlights the flavors of the Iberian Peninsula, and a variety of enriching activities and entertainment, including wine tastings and cooking demonstrations, classical music performances, and expert-led discussions. It strikes the ideal balance between cultural immersion and creature comforts, allowing you to fully enjoy the Douro Valley's many attractions without sacrificing any comfort or sophistication.

Ultimately, a Douro River cruise provides a truly transformative travel experience. By giving in to the river's gentle rhythms and allowing yourself to be enveloped by the valley's timeless allure, you'll return home with indelible memories, a deeper appreciation for Portugal's heritage, and a desire to one day retrace your steps along this truly enchanting waterway. So, why not answer the Douro's siren call and embark on a once-in-a-lifetime adventure? I can assure you that it will leave an impression on your heart and mind for many years to come.

15 Fascinating Facts About the Douro River

1. Ancient Origins: The Douro River has its origins dating back over 2 million years, making it one of the oldest rivers in Europe. Its name is derived from the Roman "Durius", meaning "golden" - a reference to the river's historic role in the gold mining industry.

2. UNESCO World Heritage: In 2001, the Douro Wine Region, which encompasses the Douro River Valley, was designated a UNESCO World Heritage site in recognition of its outstanding universal value as an evolving, traditional wine-producing region.

3. World's Oldest Demarcated Wine Region: The Douro Valley is home to the world's oldest demarcated wine region, having been officially delimited and regulated by the Marquis of Pombal in 1756. This makes it older than the Bordeaux wine region in France.

4. Cinematic Landscapes: The Douro River winds its way through some of the most dramatically beautiful landscapes in Europe, with steep, terraced vineyards cascading down schist cliffs and picturesque villages nestled along the riverbanks. It's no wonder the region has served as a backdrop for numerous films.

5. Port Wine Capital: The city of Porto, situated at the mouth of the Douro River, is renowned as the historic capital of Portugal's famous Port wine industry. This fortified wine has been produced in the Douro Valley for centuries and is a quintessential part of the region's identity.

6. Rugged Viticulture: Grape-growing in the Douro Valley is an immense challenge, with vineyards planted on vertiginous, hand-terraced slopes that can reach gradients of up to 45 degrees. This extreme terrain has forced wine producers to develop innovative cultivation techniques.

7. Douro Rabelo Boats: The traditional flat-bottomed boats known as Douro Rabelos were once used to transport barrels of Port wine down the river from the quintas (wine estates) to the port houses in Porto. While no longer in commercial use, they remain an iconic symbol of the Douro's viticultural heritage.

8. Railway Engineering Feat: The Douro Line railway, which runs along the northern bank of the river, is considered an outstanding engineering achievement. Completed in 1887, the line required the construction of 33 tunnels and 30 bridges to navigate the Douro's rugged terrain.

9. Migratory Fish: The Douro River is home to a number of migratory fish species, including the critically endangered Atlantic sturgeon and the Iberian roach. Conservation efforts are underway to protect these unique aquatic populations.

10. Hydroelectric Power: The Douro River is an important source of hydroelectric power for Portugal, with a number of dams and power plants located along its course, including the iconic Crestuma-Lever Dam.

11. Birdwatching Haven: The Douro Valley provides a habitat for a diverse array of bird species, making it a popular destination for birdwatchers. Notable residents

include the Bonelli's eagle, the black stork, and the Iberian chiffchaff.

12. Almond Blossom Season: Each spring, the Douro Valley's almond trees burst into bloom, creating a stunning natural spectacle that attracts visitors from around the world to witness the enchanting pink and white flowers.

13. Olive Oil Production: In addition to its world-famous wines, the Douro Valley is also renowned for its high-quality extra virgin olive oil, produced from the region's centuries-old olive groves.

14. Prehistoric Rock Art: The Douro Valley is home to some of the world's oldest known examples of rock art, with ancient paintings and carvings dating back thousands of years found in various sites along the river.

15. Douro International Natural Park: Straddling the border between Portugal and Spain, the Douro International Natural Park protects the natural ecosystems and biodiversity of the Douro River as it flows through a rugged, mountainous region.

CHAPTER 2.

PLANNING YOUR Douro RIVER CRUISE

Best Time of Year to Visit

Based on my experience in cruising Douro River, I can say with confidence that the best time to plan your journey along this enchanting waterway truly depends on your particular interests and travel preferences. The Douro Valley is a region that offers a wealth of seasonal delights, each with its own unique charm and attractions.

Summer is an excellent time to immerse yourself in the Douro's vibrant cultural festivities. From June to August, the valley is alive with vibrant festivals and celebrations that highlight the region's rich folkloric traditions. In June, the historic city of Porto hosts the iconic Festa de São João, a raucous all-night street party with live music, fireworks, and traditional sardine and vinho verde dinners. Elsewhere in the valley, village festivals celebrate everything from the grape harvest to local patron saints, giving you the opportunity to mingle with locals and learn about the Douro's long-standing traditions.

The summer season also provides ideal conditions for exploring the Douro's picturesque landscapes. With long, sunny days and average temperatures in the mid to high 20s Celsius, it's the ideal time to hike through the terraced vineyards, kayak down the river, or simply relax on the deck of your river cruise ship as the scenery passes by. Just keep in mind that this is the Douro's peak tourism season, so book your trip early to get the best deals and availability.

Those looking for a more peaceful and contemplative Douro experience may want to visit during the shoulder seasons of spring and autumn. In the spring, the valley is blanketed in a tapestry of vibrant wildflowers, and the almond trees blossom, creating a breathtaking natural spectacle. The temperatures are mild, making it ideal for more leisurely activities such as wine tastings, town walks, and scenic river cruises. Meanwhile, autumn brings the drama of grape harvest, as vineyards transform into a patchwork of golds, reds, and russets. This is also an excellent time to enjoy the Douro's world-famous Port wines, as the new vintage is being laid down in the region's historic wine cellars.

However, keep in mind that the weather in the Douro Valley can vary greatly even within the same season. Spring and autumn, in particular, can experience rapid temperature and precipitation changes, so pack layers and be prepared for anything. While quieter, the winter months can be cold and wet, with river cruise schedules potentially disrupted due to high water levels or other weather-related factors.

Finally, the best time to visit the Douro Valley will depend on your personal preferences and the experiences you want to have. I encourage you to carefully consider the advantages and disadvantages of each season, and to be flexible in your planning to accommodate any unexpected weather conditions. Wherever and whenever you decide to visit this captivating region, I'm confident you'll be rewarded with unforgettable memories and a deeper appreciation for the Douro's timeless allure.

Choosing a Cruise Line and Itinerary

When it comes to planning the perfect Douro River cruise, the selection of a suitable cruise line and itinerary is of paramount importance. As an experienced guide along this enchanting waterway, I've had the privilege of working with a wide range of operators, each offering their own unique take on the Douro experience. Based on this extensive knowledge, I'm pleased to offer the following insights and recommendations to help you make the most informed decision for your upcoming journey.

First and foremost, I would recommend that you prioritize cruise lines that specialize in navigating the Douro River over those that only include it as a stop on a larger European itinerary. These expert operators will not only be intimately familiar with the river's unique geography and logistical challenges, but they will also be better equipped to provide an immersive, enriching experience that truly reflects the Douro's cultural and natural wonders.

Uniworld, AmaWaterways, Scenic, and Viking are among the most reputable and respected cruise lines on the Douro River. These companies have made significant investments in the development of custom-designed river ships that are ideal for the Douro's narrower, sometimes shallower, waterways, ensuring a smooth and comfortable journey. Furthermore, their itineraries are carefully designed to highlight the best of the Douro Valley, with plenty of opportunities for cultural immersion, wine tasting, and off-the-beaten-path exploration.

When evaluating specific itineraries, I recommend looking for voyages that provide a balanced mix of time spent on the river and onshore. While scenic cruising is undeniably enjoyable, the true essence of the Douro Valley can be found in its historic towns, vineyard-clad hillsides, and family-run wine estates. Look for itineraries that include enough time in destinations like Porto, Régua, Pinhão, and Salamanca, Spain, to explore the region's history, architecture, and world-renowned viticulture.

It's also important to consider the length of the cruise. While shorter 4-7 night itineraries can provide a tantalizing taste of the Douro, I believe the best experience is found on longer 7-14 night voyages. These longer journeys not only allow you to cover more ground along the river, but they also give you the time and space to truly immerse yourself in the valley's relaxed pace and rich cultural tapestry.

One final piece of advice: keep water levels in mind when booking your Douro River cruise. Because the river is prone to seasonal fluctuations, certain sections may become impassable during times of high or low water. Reputable cruise lines will have contingency plans in place, such as coach transfers or alternative itineraries, but it is always a good idea to book with some flexibility in case you need to change your itinerary.

Ultimately, the Douro River cruise that is best for you will be determined by your personal interests, budget, and travel style. However, by keeping these key considerations in mind and working with a cruise line that specializes in this incredible destination, I am confident you will embark on a journey that will leave an indelible mark on your heart and mind. So start planning your dream Douro adventure today - the river is calling, and it's time to answer the siren.

Duration of Cruise Trips

When it comes to planning the perfect Douro River cruise, the question of trip duration is a crucial consideration that can have a significant impact on the overall quality and depth of your experience. As an expert guide along this enchanting waterway, I've had the privilege of accompanying travellers on a wide range of Douro River cruises, from short, introductory journeys to more immersive, extended voyages. Drawing on this wealth of experience, I'm pleased to offer the following insights and recommendations to help you determine the optimal trip length for your upcoming adventure.

For first-time visitors to the Douro Valley or those with limited time, I recommend a four- to seven-night cruise itinerary. These shorter voyages offer an excellent introduction to the region's highlights, allowing you to enjoy scenic cruising along the river, explore the historic city of Porto, and visit a number of iconic Douro Valley towns and wine estates. Itineraries in this duration range typically focus on the western, more accessible stretch of the river, from Porto upriver to the scenic town of Pinhão.

While these shorter cruises are a convenient and cost-effective way to discover the Douro, I would warn that they can occasionally feel rushed, leaving little room for spontaneity or in-depth exploration. The pace can feel hurried, with a greater emphasis on efficiently ticking off the major sights rather than fully immersing yourself in the region's unhurried rhythms and rich cultural tapestry.

For those looking for a more comprehensive and leisurely Douro experience, I strongly recommend booking a 7 to 14-night cruise itinerary. These extended voyages allow you to not only explore a larger portion of the river, but also learn more about the Douro Valley's history, traditions, and daily life. Longer itineraries usually include visits to a broader range of towns and villages, from the UNESCO-designated city of Porto to the remote, vineyard-draped hillsides further upstream.

Crucially, these extended cruises allow you to fully immerse yourself in the Douro's captivating atmosphere. Rather than feeling rushed, you'll be able to appreciate the ever-changing landscape, partake in wine tastings and culinary experiences, and form meaningful connections with the locals. Many of these itineraries include excursions to the neighboring Salamanca region of Spain, broadening your cultural horizons even further.

Of course, the ideal trip duration will ultimately be determined by your personal travel preferences, interests, and available time. Those looking for a more relaxed, contemplative experience may find that 10 to 14 nights is ideal, whereas more active travelers may be perfectly satisfied with a compact 4 or 5-night cruise. Regardless of your preference, I would advise you to resist the temptation to book the shortest possible duration, as this may leave you feeling as if you've only scratched the surface of this incredible destination.

Finally, the Douro River is a region that rewards deeper exploration, and the more time you can devote to your cruise, the more enriching and rewarding your experience will be. So, as you begin planning your Douro adventure, I encourage you to carefully consider your options, weigh the benefits and drawbacks of various trip lengths, and select the itinerary that will allow you to fully immerse yourself in the valley's captivating charms.

Budgeting and Costs

Based on my experience in cruising Douro River, I understand that one of the most important considerations when planning your dream voyage is the question of budgeting and costs. The Douro is undoubtedly a premier European travel destination, and the river cruise experience can represent a significant investment. However, I'm here to assure you that, with a bit of careful planning and a nuanced understanding of the various factors involved, it is entirely possible to enjoy a luxurious and enriching Douro River cruise without breaking the bank.

First and foremost, you should understand that the overall cost of your Douro River cruise will be heavily influenced by the length of your trip and the level of accommodation and amenities you select. Longer cruises (7-14 nights) and higher-end river ships will typically cost more than shorter, less expensive options. However, when you consider the all-inclusive nature of these voyages, even the most luxurious Douro River cruise experiences can be extremely cost effective.

When planning your cruise budget, keep in mind the base fare, which includes your accommodations, meals, and on-board entertainment and enrichment activities. Many cruise lines include select shore excursions, such as guided tours of historic towns and wine tastings, as part of their standard package. You may need to budget for additional "à la carte" excursions, pre- and post-cruise hotel stays, and transfers.

The time of year you choose to travel will also have a significant impact on your total costs. The Douro Valley, like many popular destinations, experiences seasonal fluctuations in demand, with peak season (summer) typically commanding higher prices than shoulder seasons (spring and autumn). If your travel dates are flexible, I recommend looking into cruise options during these quieter periods, when you may be able to take advantage of lower fares and fewer crowds.

One of the most significant benefits of a Douro River cruise, in my opinion, is the all-inclusive nature of the experience, which can make it a more cost-effective option than piecing together a land itinerary. In addition to your accommodations and meals, many river cruise lines provide beer, wine, and soft drinks at lunch and dinner, as well as on-board gratuities. This can result in significant savings over the à la carte costs of a more traditional land-based holiday.

When it comes to budgeting for your shore excursions and onshore expenses, I recommend setting aside a daily per-person allowance of around €50-€100, depending on the activities you plan and your personal spending habits. This should include entrance fees, local transportation, meals ashore, and any additional shopping or tastings you want to do.

Ultimately, the total cost of your Douro River cruise will be determined by your personal travel preferences and budget. However, by working closely with a reputable cruise line, planning ahead of time, and taking advantage of any available promotions or discounts, I am confident you will be able to create an unforgettable Douro experience that fits within your budget. So don't be put off by the perceived exclusivity of this remarkable destination; with some careful planning, the Douro's charms can be within reach of travelers of all means.

CHAPTER 3.

GETTING TO THE DOURO RIVER

Flying into Porto or other Nearby Airports

When it comes to reaching the Douro River Valley, the most convenient and accessible gateway is undoubtedly the historic city of Porto. As the traditional heart of Portugal's renowned Port wine industry and a UNESCO World Heritage site in its own right, Porto serves as the natural starting point for the majority of Douro River cruises. However, for the discerning traveller, there are a number of other nearby airport options worth considering, each with its own unique advantages.

For those flying in from North America, Europe, or further afield, the Francisco Sá Carneiro Airport (OPO), located just 11 km north of central Porto, is the obvious choice. This modern, well-connected international hub offers direct flights from a wide range of major cities, making it a seamless and efficient point of entry. Upon arrival, you'll find ample public transportation options, including metro, bus, and taxi services, to whisk you directly to your Douro River cruise embarkation point or hotel in downtown Porto.

One word of caution, however: as a popular tourist destination, Porto's airport can become congested, particularly during peak travel seasons. I recommend giving yourself plenty of time to navigate airport procedures, as well as accounting for potential delays due to weather or other operational factors. Booking airport transfers or private car services through your cruise line or hotel can be a good investment to ensure a stress-free arrival.

Alternatively, savvy travelers may want to consider flying into other nearby airports with easy access to the Douro Valley. One such option is Spain's Vitoria Airport (VIT), which is just across the border from the Douro region. While it does not have the same extensive international route network as Porto, this smaller regional airport may be an appealing option for those looking to avoid the crowds and potential delays at the larger hub. The scenic drive from Vitoria to the heart of the Douro Valley takes about two hours.

Another intriguing option is Salamanca Airport (SLM), which is located just across the Spanish border and about 2 hours from the Douro. This airport not only serves as a gateway to the Douro but also provides easy access to the historic university city of Salamanca, a UNESCO World Heritage site and a popular side excursion for many Douro river cruises. The only possible disadvantage is that transfer times to Douro River embarkation points may be slightly longer than from Portuguese airports.

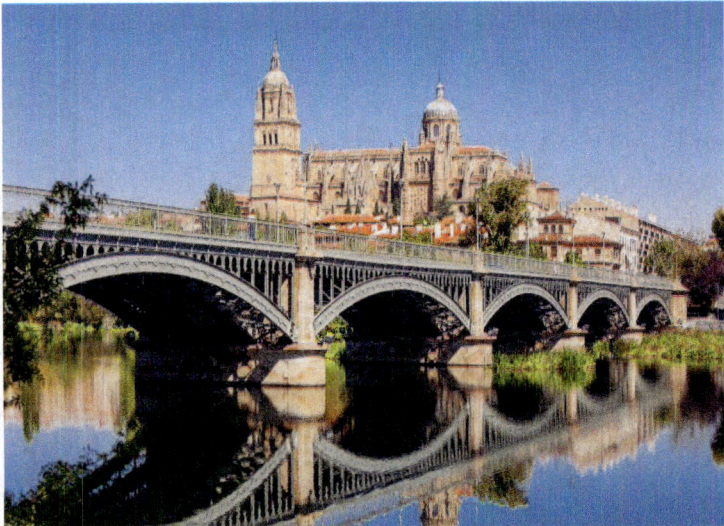

Whichever airport you choose, I strongly advise you to book your flights well in advance, as availability and fares can fluctuate significantly, particularly during peak travel periods. Furthermore, make sure to carefully coordinate your arrival and departure times with your Douro River cruise itinerary, allowing plenty of time for transfers and, if necessary, pre- or post-cruise hotel accommodations.

Ultimately, the 'best' airport for your Douro River cruise journey will be determined by a number of factors, including your departure point, budget, and travel preferences. But, regardless of which option you choose, I'm confident that with some careful planning, you'll be able to easily access this captivating region and embark on an unforgettable journey along the UNESCO-protected Douro River.

Train, Bus, and Private Transfer Options

In addition to the convenient air travel options available for reaching the Douro River Valley, there are several other ground transportation modes worth considering, each with its own distinct advantages and considerations. As an experienced guide intimately familiar with the region, I'm pleased to offer the following insights and recommendations to help you navigate the best way to get yourself and your luggage from your arrival point to your Douro River cruise embarkation.

The train is a great option for people looking for a more picturesque and engaging travel experience. Winding through some of the most dramatic landscapes in the valley, the Douro Line railway is regarded as an engineering marvel. It runs along the northern bank of the river. Not only does taking this historic rail trip lessen your environmental impact, but it also gives you a captivating view of the terraced vineyards, ancient quintas, and quaint riverside towns that line the Douro.

The town of Régua, a major port of call for numerous Douro River cruises, is home to the main train station serving the Douro region. From here, it's a relatively quick transfer (about 30 minutes) to the Douro voyage's usual starting point, the historic city of Porto. If you would rather, you can arrange for a private transfer or taxi to take you to the cruise embarkation point after taking the train straight to Porto.

But be advised: there is a chance that the Douro Line won't operate as planned, especially during bad weather or high water levels. Even though the rail operator usually has backup plans, it's a good idea to allow some leeway in your travel itinerary to accommodate for any unexpected delays or detours.

Make reservations for a private transfer service if you'd like ground transportation that is more convenient and direct. This service is provided by numerous Douro River cruise lines and hotels; it can be added to your overall travel package or offered separately. A private transfer has many benefits, including a smooth, door-to-door experience and a professional driver who will take care of your luggage and lead you directly to your destination. This can prove particularly advantageous in situations where you are traveling in a group or carrying a substantial amount of luggage.

However, since private transfers are typically more costly, it's important to consider your overall travel budget in addition to the convenience factor. Make sure to ask questions about amenities, vehicle size, and any additional costs—like those for waiting times or stops en route—as you investigate different transfer companies.

Regional bus services can also be a practical and frequently beautiful way for travelers on a tighter budget to get to the Douro River Valley. Regular routes connecting major cities like Porto, Régua, and Pinhão are run by companies like Rede Expressos and Renex, and their fares are usually far less expensive than private transfers. The trade-off is that bus trips may take longer and involve more stops along the route, making them less direct.

The ideal mode of ground transportation for your Douro River cruise will ultimately depend on a number of factors, such as your travel preferences, group size, budget, and luggage requirements. I would strongly advise you to carefully consider the advantages and disadvantages of each choice, and to consult with your cruise line or travel agent to find the most convenient and effective route to reach the magical beaches of the Douro. You'll have an amazing river cruise experience if you put in a little careful planning.

Tips for Arriving and Embarkation

While the journey to the Douro Valley is often a highlight in itself, the final steps of arriving at your cruise embarkation point and boarding your ship can sometimes be the source of a bit of uncertainty or stress. To help ensure a smooth and seamless transition into your Douro River cruise experience, I'm pleased to offer the following essential tips and recommendations.

First and foremost, I cannot overstate the importance of arriving at your embarkation point with plenty of time to spare. Weather and water levels in the Douro River region can change quickly, and cruise lines must frequently adjust their schedules and procedures to account for this. Giving yourself a generous buffer - I typically recommend arriving at least 2 hours before your scheduled departure - allows you to deal with any unexpected delays or logistical challenges without feeling rushed or anxious.

Upon arrival at your cruise ship's docking location, whether in the heart of historic Porto or a more remote riverside town, you should follow the clear signage and instructions provided by your cruise line. Cruise representatives will greet you, assist with your luggage, and walk you through the embarkation process. To expedite your boarding, I recommend keeping your passport, cruise documentation, and any necessary health forms readily available.

One tip I like to give to my guests is to take a moment before stepping aboard to take in your surroundings and appreciate the sheer beauty of the Douro Valley that stretches out before you. This is when your journey's anticipation truly comes to life, and you may experience a deep sense of excitement and wonder. Accept it - this is the beginning of an unforgettable adventure!

When you board your ship, you will be greeted by the attentive crew, who will show you around your stateroom, on-board facilities, and vessel layout. I'd recommend that you familiarize yourself with the ship's key areas, such as the lounge, dining room, and any upper-deck observation areas, so that you can make the most of your time on the water.

Finally, if you arrive early and have some free time before departing, consider taking a walk along the riverfront promenade or exploring the area around your embarkation point. This is an excellent opportunity to soak up the local atmosphere, visit a riverside café, or pick up any last-minute cruise essentials.

By following these simple tips and enjoying the excitement of your Douro River cruise, I am confident you will have an unforgettable journey along this UNESCO-protected waterway. So pack your bags, double-check your travel documents, and prepare to immerse yourself in the allure of the Douro Valley - the river is calling, and it's time to heed its siren call.

CHAPTER 4.

ON BOARD THE CRUISE SHIP

Cabin Types and Amenities

When it comes to the accommodations aboard Douro River cruise ships, the options range from cozy and comfortable to truly opulent, catering to a wide variety of traveller preferences and budgets. As an experienced guide along this enchanting waterway, I'm pleased to provide you with a comprehensive overview of the different cabin categories and their associated amenities, to help you select the perfect home-away-from-home for your upcoming journey.

On most Douro River cruise ships, the entry-level cabin category is the Standard or Classic cabin. These relatively small staterooms, ranging from 150 to 200 square feet, are tastefully decorated with necessary furnishings and amenities. The room's centerpiece is a comfortable double or twin bed configuration, ensuring a restful night's sleep after a day of immersive exploration ashore. The en-suite bathroom with shower is a welcome respite for freshening up, and the small seating area provides a cozy space to relax.

One feature I particularly like about the Standard cabins is the inclusion of large, panoramic windows that allow you to enjoy the ever-changing views of the Douro Valley while relaxing in your room. These panoramic windows are a game changer because they provide a seamless connection to the breathtaking landscapes that line the river's banks, increasing the overall sense of immersion in your surroundings. However, I would avoid booking a cabin with a "French balcony" - a narrow, Juliet-style railing that, while visually appealing, provides little in the way of usable outdoor space.

The next cabin category to consider is the Deluxe or Balcony cabin, which offers a little more space and amenities. These staterooms, which range in size from 180 to 250 square feet, have a more spacious layout and include a private, full-size balcony. This tranquil outdoor oasis, complete with comfortable seating, offers the ideal vantage point from which to enjoy the Douro's breathtaking scenery as it passes by. Whether you're sipping your morning coffee, enjoying a glass of local port in the evening, or simply admiring the ever-changing scenery, the private balcony is a game changer, elevating your overall connection to the river.

The Deluxe cabins' increased square footage also allows for a larger bathroom and, in some cases, a separate living/sitting area. This additional space creates a more luxurious and comfortable environment, ideal for those looking to fully immerse themselves in the Douro River experience. I believe that the Deluxe cabins strike an excellent balance of comfort, privacy, and value, making them an excellent choice for many travelers.

The Suite categories are the pinnacle of Douro River cruise accommodations, with sizes ranging from 300 to 450 square feet. These palatial staterooms provide an unprecedented level of space and luxury, with separate living and sleeping areas, expansive balconies, and a plethora of premium amenities. Suites may also include perks like dedicated butler service, free laundry, and priority access to shore excursions.

The vast amount of space in the Suite categories makes for a truly indulgent and relaxing experience. The separate living and sleeping areas create a wonderful sense of separation between your private sanctuary and the ship's more public spaces, while the expansive balconies provide an exclusive front-row seat to the Douro Valley's breathtaking scenery. These additional luxuries, combined with attentive butler service and priority access to shore excursions, make the Suite experience truly memorable.

Regardless of which cabin category you choose, I am confident that the attention to detail, quality of furnishings, and overall comfort level on Douro River cruise ships will exceed your expectations. The guiding principle of these vessels is to provide a luxurious but intimate home base from which to explore this fascinating region. With that in mind, I recommend that you choose the cabin that best fits your travel style, budget, and personal preferences - the Douro is waiting to be discovered, and your floating home will be an important part of the journey.

Dining and Cuisine

One of the true highlights of any Douro River cruise is the exceptional quality and diverse range of culinary experiences that await you on board. As an avid foodie and passionate advocate for the regional gastronomy of Portugal, I'm delighted to share my insights on the dining and cuisine you can expect to enjoy during your journey along this captivating waterway.

The main restaurant serves exquisitely prepared meals, which are central to the on-board dining experience. The chefs aboard Douro River cruise ships strive to showcase the best of Portuguese and Mediterranean-inspired cuisine while adhering to the highest quality and presentation standards. Consider fresh, locally sourced ingredients, expertly crafted dishes, and a carefully curated wine list to accompany each course.

Many Douro River cruise lines take pride in celebrating the Douro Valley's regional specialties. From the world-renowned Port wines to the hearty, rustic stews and abundance of fresh seafood, the menus on board these vessels are designed to immerse you in the flavors and culinary traditions of this remarkable destination. Classic dishes such as Bacalhau à Brás (salted cod with eggs and potatoes) and Caldo Verde (the iconic Portuguese kale and potato soup) are common, as are more modern interpretations of local delicacies.

In addition to the main dining room, many Douro River cruise ships also offer a variety of alternative dining venues and experiences to cater to your evolving tastes and preferences throughout your voyage. These might include:

Specialty Restaurants: Intimate, reservation-only venues that showcase the talents of the on-board culinary team through tasting menus or thematic dining experiences.

Alfresco Dining: Casual, open-air eateries where you can enjoy lighter fare and breathtaking views of the Douro's passing landscapes.

Afternoon Tea Service: A timeless tradition that allows you to indulge in freshly baked pastries, finger sandwiches, and, of course, a selection of premium teas.

Late-Night Snacks: For those times when you need a little something to satisfy your cravings after a day of exploration, many ships offer a variety of light bites and nightcaps.

Regardless of which dining option you choose, you can be confident that the level of service, attention to detail, and overall quality will be consistently high. The crew on these ships takes great pride in ensuring that each meal is a true culinary adventure, seamlessly blending traditional flavors with modern flair.

As you plan your Douro River cruise, I recommend inquiring about any special dietary requirements or preferences you may have, as the on-board culinary teams are skilled at catering to a wide range of needs, including vegetarian, vegan, gluten-free, and halal. With a little advance notice, they'll be happy to accommodate your specific preferences and ensure that you thoroughly enjoy every bite of your voyage.

Entertainment and Onboard Activities

While the Douro River itself and the captivating scenery that lines its banks are undoubtedly the main draw of a Douro River cruise, the on-board entertainment and activities offered by these ships play a vital role in creating a truly immersive and enriching experience for guests. As an experienced guide, I'm delighted to share insights into the diverse array of options available to you during your time on the water.

The ship's knowledgeable and engaging crew hosts daily lectures, presentations, and cultural performances, which are central to the on-board entertainment experience. These educational and cultural offerings aim to provide deeper insights into the Douro Valley's history, art, and traditions, as well as those of Portugal as a whole. You might find yourself attending a talk about the region's legendary Port wine production, taking a hands-on Portuguese language lesson, or watching a lively folkloric dance performance.

In addition to these enrichment activities, Douro River cruise ships provide a wide range of recreational activities to keep you entertained and engaged throughout your journey. Many vessels have well-equipped fitness centers, which are ideal for keeping up with your workout routine while on the road. For those who prefer a more leisurely approach to physical activity, the sun decks and outdoor walking tracks offer plenty of opportunities for taking gentle strolls and admiring the breathtaking riverside views.

For those seeking relaxation, the on-board spas are a true highlight, offering a tempting menu of soothing treatments and therapies. Imagine enjoying a rejuvenating massage, a revitalizing facial, or a stress-relieving soak in the hot tub while admiring the ever-changing Douro landscape. It's the ideal way to relax and recharge after a day of immersive exploration ashore.

Of course, no Douro River cruise would be complete without sampling the region's renowned cuisine and beverages. Many ships have dedicated wine lounges or tasting rooms where you can sample the best vintages from the Douro's renowned vineyards with the help of expert sommeliers. Cooking demonstrations and hands-on classes also allow you to delve deeper into the secrets of Portuguese cuisine while improving your own culinary skills.

For those looking for a more social atmosphere, the on-board lounges and bars offer inviting spaces to mingle with fellow passengers, listen to live music or entertainment, and perhaps even participate in a game of trivia or another group activity. These convivial gatherings are frequently a highlight for guests, fostering a sense of community and leaving lasting memories of their Douro River cruise.

Regardless of your personal interests or preferences, I am confident that the entertainment and activity options available on Douro River cruise ships will provide you with plenty of opportunities to enrich your journey and make the most of your time on the water. Whether you're looking for enrichment, relaxation, or simply the opportunity to immerse yourself in the region's vibrant culture, the on-board experience will exceed your expectations.

Shore Excursions and Land Exploration

A Douro River cruise is certainly made more enjoyable by the shore excursions and land-based explorations that are provided; however, the Douro River itself and the breathtaking scenery that adorns its banks are the cruise's true draws. I'm happy to share my knowledge of the wide range of on-shore activities and immersive experiences that you can partake in while visiting the Douro Valley as an experienced guide.

One of the hallmarks of a Douro River cruise is the opportunity to disembark the ship and venture into the stunning landscapes, historic towns, and cultural heart of this UNESCO-protected region. The carefully curated shore excursion programs offered by cruise lines are designed to provide guests with a profound and multifaceted understanding of the Douro's unique identity.

Whether you are drawn to the region's renowned wineries and vineyards, captivated by the architectural wonders of its historic cities, or eager to learn about local traditions and folkways, there is an excursion to suit every interest and activity level. Explore Pinhão's riverside streets, admire its iconic azulejo-tiled buildings, or visit a family-owned Quinta to learn about the complex process of producing Port wine.

For more adventurous travelers, the shore excursion program frequently includes opportunities for active pursuits, such as guided hikes through the Douro's dramatic landscapes or kayaking along the river's tranquil waters. These immersive, hands-on experiences offer an unparalleled connection to the breathtaking natural beauty of this region.

In addition to structured shore excursions, many Douro River cruise lines allow guests to explore on their own, providing maps, recommendations, and logistical support to ensure a smooth and enriching independent journey. This freedom allows you to explore at your own pace, discovering hidden treasures and fully immersing yourself in the local culture.

One piece of advice I frequently give my guests is to embrace the art of slow travel while on shore. Rather than rushing from one attraction to the next, take the time to relax in the town squares, chat with the friendly locals, and simply absorb the rhythms of daily life in the Douro Valley. In these unhurried moments, the true essence of the region often shines through.

Regardless of how you spend your time on shore, I am confident that the immersive experiences and cultural insights provided by Douro River cruise excursions will be a highlight of your trip. These land-based excursions are the ideal complement to the tranquil river cruising, allowing you to gain a deep and multifaceted understanding of this captivating corner of Portugal.

CHAPTER 5.

EXPLORING PORTO

Ribeira Historic Centre

As you disembark your Douro River cruise and set foot in the enchanting city of Porto, one of the must-visit destinations that will undoubtedly captivate your senses is the Ribeira Historic Centre. This UNESCO World Heritage Site, nestled along the riverbanks, is a veritable jewel in the crown of this captivating Portuguese destination, brimming with centuries-old charm, cultural riches, and an irresistible allure that will leave a lasting impression.

The Ribeira district is the heart and soul of historic Porto, a labyrinth of narrow, winding streets and picturesque squares that bear witness to the city's rich history. Walking through this enthralling neighborhood, you'll notice the striking contrast of towering, colorful townhouses leaning precariously over the Douro River, their bold facades adorned with intricate azulejo tiles that gleam in the sunlight. This harmonious blend of vernacular architecture and the ever-present waterway creates a stunning visual tapestry.

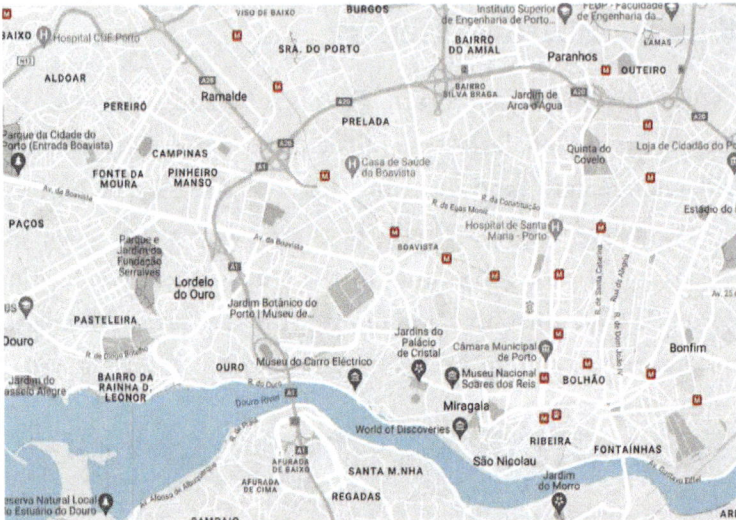

As you wander the charming alleyways, I recommend taking your time and soaking up the authentic atmosphere that pervades every corner of the Ribeira. Take a moment to admire the intricate ironwork on the balconies, the weathered limestone facades, and the occasional glimpse of the river through the narrow passageways. In these unhurried moments, the true essence of this historic precinct often emerges, transporting you to a bygone era.

One of the Ribeira's undisputed highlights is the bustling Praça da Ribeira, which serves as the district's central hub. Here, you'll find a fascinating fusion of local life, with street performers entertaining the crowds, artisanal shops and galleries beckoning you to explore their wares, and a plethora of inviting cafés and restaurants serving traditional Portuguese cuisine. I'd recommend taking some time to relax, sip on a refreshing glass of vinho verde, and people-watch, letting the square's energy wash over you.

As you continue to explore the Ribeira, keep an eye out for the iconic Cais da Ribeira, a picturesque riverside promenade that runs along the Douro. This scenic walkway provides breathtaking views of the Dom Luís I Bridge, a magnificent twin-deck structure that spans the river, as well as the charming traditional boats known as rabelos, which were once used to transport the famous Port wine from the Douro Valley.

Cais da Ribeira

One word of caution, however: the Ribeira's historical charm and unparalleled setting have made it a popular destination for both tourists and locals. As a result, the area can get quite crowded, particularly during peak tourist seasons. To fully immerse yourself in the district's enchanting atmosphere, I recommend going in the early morning or late afternoon, when the crowds are thinner and the light casts a warm, golden glow on the historic buildings.

Regardless of when you visit the Ribeira, I am confident that this captivating district will leave an indelible impression on your Douro River cruise adventure. The seamless blend of cultural heritage, architectural splendour, and vibrant local energy results in a truly immersive and unforgettable experience that will leave you wanting to return to this enchanting corner of Portugal.

Port Wine Cellars

No visit to Porto would be complete without an in-depth exploration of the city's world-renowned Port wine heritage. As the historic heart of this celebrated fortified wine's production, Porto is home to a remarkable collection of atmospheric Port wine cellars that offer visitors a captivating glimpse into the centuries-old traditions and meticulous craftsmanship that have made Port a global phenomenon.

The Vila Nova de Gaia district, located just across the iconic Douro River from the Ribeira Historic Centre, is one of the most popular Port wine destinations in Porto. This vibrant neighborhood is dotted with the grand, story-filled cellars of the most prestigious Port wine houses, each inviting visitors to delve into the storied history of this quintessential Portuguese libation.

I would strongly advise you to devote a significant portion of your time in Porto to exploring these captivating cellars, as the opportunity to not only sample the world's finest Ports but also gain a better understanding of the region's viticultural heritage is truly unique. Many of the cellars provide comprehensive guided tours that take visitors through the various stages of Port production, from grape harvest and fermentation to the complex blending and ageing processes that give each vintage its distinct character.

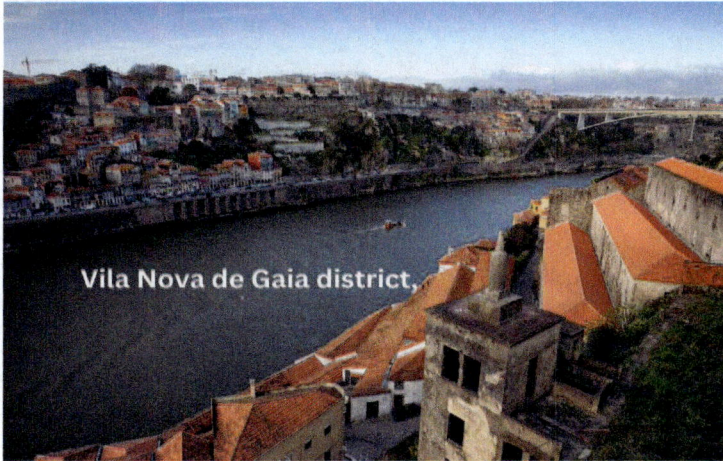

Vila Nova de Gaia district,

One of the highlights of these tours is the opportunity to enter the cavernous, dimly lit barrel rooms, where row after row of ancient, weathered oak casks slumber, gradually imparting their oaky notes and velvety textures to the precious liquid within. The reverent silence that pervades these atmospheric spaces is truly captivating, evoking a sense of timelessness and the enduring traditions passed down through generations of Port artisans.

Of course, no visit to a Port wine cellar is complete without a tasting, and Porto has some truly world-class options. Whether you choose a guided tasting that allows you to sample a variety of styles, from bold, ruby-hued Ports to luscious, amber-colored Tawnies, or you prefer to delve into the nuances of a single exceptional vintage, your palate will be delighted and enlightened.

I would, however, advise caution: with so many renowned Port houses to choose from, it is easy to become overwhelmed by the sheer number of options. My advice would be to do your research ahead of time, focusing on the cellars with the most compelling histories, knowledgeable and engaging tour guides, and the best reputations for quality. A little advance planning will help you make the most of your Port-tasting experience while in Porto.

In addition to guided tours and tastings, many Port wine cellars sell bottles to take home, allowing you to explore this captivating libation long after your Douro River cruise has ended. I would recommend that you speak with the knowledgeable staff about the best options for your specific preferences and budget, as they will be able to provide expert recommendations and guidance.

Finally, a deep dive into the world of Port wine is a must-do during any visit to Porto, as it not only allows you to savor one of Portugal's most celebrated culinary exports, but it also provides a glimpse into the rich history, traditions, and artistry that have defined this remarkable region for centuries. Exploring the Port wine cellars with a little planning and an open palate will undoubtedly be a highlight of your Douro River cruise.

Bridges and Views of the City

As you wander the captivating streets and historic neighbourhoods of Porto, your gaze will inevitably be drawn skyward, towards the magnificent bridges that span the mighty Douro River, linking the city's two banks and offering some of the most breathtaking vantage points from which to admire this UNESCO World Heritage site.

Chief among Porto's iconic bridges is the magnificent **Ponte Dom Luís I,** a true engineering marvel that has become one of the city's most recognisable landmarks. Designed by the renowned French architect Gustave Eiffel (of Eiffel Tower fame), this impressive, double-decker iron bridge is a testament to the city's 19th-century industrial prowess, as well as its enduring architectural brilliance.

Ponte Dom Luís I

I would highly recommend taking the time to not only admire this iconic structure from the riverbanks but also to ascend to the upper level, which provides unparalleled, panoramic views over the entire Douro River valley. The journey to the top, whether by stairs or the included elevator, is well worth the effort, as it affords you the opportunity to gaze out over the terracotta rooftops of the Ribeira district, the charming traditional boats (rabelos) plying the river's waters, and the verdant hills that rise majestically on the opposite shore.

Another essential bridge to explore during your time in Porto is the **Ponte de Arrábida,** a more modern, concrete structure that nonetheless commands attention with its elegant, arched design and stunning setting. While not as iconic as the Ponte Dom Luís I, the Ponte de Arrábida offers a unique vantage point, allowing you to admire the city's historic core from a slightly different angle. I would suggest timing your visit to coincide with the golden hour, when the soft, warm light creates a truly magical atmosphere and accentuates the rich, earthy tones of Porto's architecture.

In addition to these two celebrated bridges, Porto is also home to several other impressive river crossings, each with its own distinct character and charm. The **Ponte do Infante,** for instance, features a sleek, contemporary design that complements the city's more modern neighbourhoods, while the historic Ponte da Arrábida, with its graceful, single-arch structure, provides a wonderful opportunity to step back in time and imagine the city's past.

No matter which bridges you choose to explore, I can assure you that the views they offer will be truly awe-inspiring. The ability to gaze out over the Douro River, with its meandering course and the undulating hills that frame the city, is an essential component of any visit to Porto, granting you a bird's-eye perspective on this captivating destination.

I would, however, offer a word of caution: the bridges, particularly the Ponte Dom Luís I, can become quite crowded, especially during peak tourist seasons. To avoid the masses and truly savour the tranquility of these remarkable vantage points, I would recommend visiting either early in the morning or later in the evening, when the crowds tend to be thinner. This will allow you to fully immerse yourself in the stunning views and the peaceful ambiance that permeates these iconic landmarks.

Ultimately, Porto's bridges are essential elements of the city's distinct identity and aesthetic fabric rather than just useful buildings. You will be treated to some of the most breathtaking views imaginable as you explore these amazing crossings, and you will also get a deeper understanding of Porto's rich history, architectural legacy, and enduring spirit. You will undoubtedly be inspired to return time and time again to this alluring city by this unforgettable experience.

CHAPTER 6.

DISCOVERING RÉGUA

Douro Museum

As your Douro River cruise glides into the quaint town of Régua, one of the must-visit destinations that will undoubtedly captivate your attention is the remarkable Douro Museum. This acclaimed institution, nestled along the riverbanks, offers visitors a profound and multifaceted exploration of the Douro Valley's rich heritage, serving as a veritable gateway to understanding the unique cultural, historical, and environmental identity of this UNESCO-protected region.

The Douro Museum's architectural design, a striking modern structure that seamlessly integrates with the surrounding landscape, is an alluring draw in itself, piquing the curiosity of all who lay eyes upon it. However, it is the museum's extensive collection and expertly curated exhibitions that truly distinguish it as a must-see attraction during your time in Régua.

When you enter the museum, you will be immersed in the history of the Douro Valley, from a rugged, remote region to a globally recognized viticultural powerhouse and UNESCO World Heritage site. The meticulously designed galleries take visitors through the region's geological formation, the evolution of its iconic terraced vineyards, and the centuries-old Port wine production traditions that define the Douro's cultural identity.

One of the highlights of the Douro Museum experience is the opportunity to learn about the intricate process of making Port wine, from the meticulous grape harvest to the complex blending and ageing techniques that transform these humble fruits into the world's most celebrated fortified wines. Multimedia displays, interactive exhibits, and even opportunities to participate in tastings and workshops bring this captivating story to life in a completely immersive and engaging way.

However, the scope of the Douro Museum extends far beyond the region's long-standing viticulture industry. Visitors can also explore the museum's extensive collection of ethnographic and archaeological artifacts, which shed light on the traditional livelihoods, customs, and daily lives of Douro Valley residents over the centuries. From the tools and implements used by the region's farmers and fishermen to the vibrant folk art and handicrafts passed down through generations, these exhibits provide a deep and multifaceted understanding of the Douro's cultural identity.

I would strongly advise you to spend a significant portion of your time in Régua exploring the Douro Museum, which truly serves as the central hub for understanding the complex and captivating story of this remarkable region. Whether you're a wine enthusiast, a history buff, or just someone who values cultural heritage, the museum's expertly curated experience will leave you with a deep and lasting connection to the Douro Valley.

As you plan your visit, I recommend allowing plenty of time to fully immerse yourself in the museum's offerings, as there is so much to discover. I would also recommend that you take advantage of any guided tours or special programs that may be available, as the insight and context provided by the museum's knowledgeable staff can greatly enhance the experience.

Finally, the Douro Museum exemplifies the Douro Valley's enduring spirit, serving as a center of knowledge, appreciation, and celebration for all who seek to discover the secrets of this UNESCO-protected treasure. Exploring its galleries and exhibits will undoubtedly be the highlight of your Douro River cruise.

Mateus Palace and Gardens

The stunning Mateus Palace and its immaculately kept gardens are among the true highlights that await you in the town of Régua as you continue your exploration of the Douro Valley region during your Douro River cruise. This recognizable 18th-century estate, which has come to be associated with the well-known Mateus Rosé wine, provides guests with an enthralling look at the region's illustrious past and the resilient spirit of Portuguese viticulture.

Mateus Palace

I would strongly advise spending a good deal of your time in Régua touring this amazing property because the Mateus Palace and the gardens around it are an absolute sensory extravaganza. The palace itself is a striking landmark that demands attention right away because of its recognizable Baroque architecture and striking pink façade. It invites you to travel back in time and imagine the opulence of Portugal's aristocratic past.

The immaculately kept formal gardens greet you as soon as you enter the estate and stretch out in front of the palace in an amazing display of symmetry and unspoiled beauty. You can see a range of decorative fountains, sculpted topiary, and colorful flower beds as you stroll along the well-kept hedgerows and winding pathways. These elements come together to create a veritable horticultural masterpiece. I would recommend allotting enough time to just stroll around and take in the peaceful atmosphere, stopping to marvel at the palace's famous silhouette reflected in the placid lake at the center of the garden.

Seeing the inside of the magnificent estate, which has been painstakingly restored to its former splendor and exquisitely preserved, is one of the real highlights of a visit to Mateus Palace. You'll be taken back in time to the 18th century as soon as you enter the palace through the elaborate entryway, where you can admire the opulent furnishings, the lavish interiors, and the amazing attention to detail that fills every nook and cranny of the building. I would suggest taking one of the guided tours; the staff's expertise will surely help you appreciate the rich history and the legacy of the Mateus family that permeate this amazing property even more.

The Mateus estate is home to a world-famous winery where you can learn the secrets of the fabled Mateus Rosé, in addition to the palace and gardens. I would highly recommend that you attend a tasting, where you will be able to taste not only the famous rosé but also some of the estate's other outstanding wines, and you will discover the careful viticulture and winemaking techniques that have defined the Douro Valley for centuries.

One word of caution, however: as the Mateus Palace and Gardens have become an increasingly popular destination, the property can become quite crowded, especially during the peak tourist seasons. To ensure you have the opportunity to fully immerse yourself in the serene atmosphere and the captivating history of the estate, I would recommend visiting either early in the morning or later in the afternoon, when the crowds tend to be thinner.

Ultimately, a visit to the Mateus Palace and Gardens is a must-do during your time in the Douro Valley, as it offers a seamless blend of architectural splendour, horticultural artistry, and cultural heritage that is truly unparalleled. Whether you're a history enthusiast, a garden lover, or simply someone in search of a truly immersive and enriching experience, this magnificent estate is sure to leave an indelible mark on your Douro River cruise journey.

Relax Along the Riverfront

I can't stress enough how much it would help to take some time to just relax and take in the tranquil atmosphere of the riverfront promenade while exploring the town of Régua in the Douro Valley. This charming section of the waterfront invites you to relax, re-establish a connection with nature, and take in the gentle rhythms of life along the Douro River. It provides a delightful diversion from the busy streets.

One of the true highlights of the riverfront experience is the opportunity to saunter along the beautifully landscaped walkways, which afford breathtaking vistas of the undulating, vine-clad hills that rise majestically on the opposite shore. As you meander at your own pace, pausing to admire the traditional rabelo boats bobbing in the waters or the stately bridges that span the river, you'll be struck by a profound sense of tranquility that can be difficult to find in more urban settings.

I would recommend that you set aside enough time to simply find a comfortable spot along the promenade, such as a park bench or a sun-dappled patch of grass, and allow yourself to be enveloped by the relaxing ambiance of the riverfront. Breathe deeply, sip a refreshing glass of the Douro's renowned vinho verde, and let your gaze drift across the gently flowing water; it's often in these unhurried moments that the true essence of the Douro Valley emerges.

For those looking for more activity, the riverfront promenade provides plenty of opportunities for gentle exploration, such as a leisurely stroll, a refreshing jog, or even a leisurely bike ride. The flat, well-maintained pathways are ideal for stretching your legs and taking in the breathtaking natural scenery that defines this UNESCO-protected region.

I would, however, advise you to exercise caution when wandering the riverfront, as the area can become quite popular, particularly during peak tourist season. To truly maximize your experience of peace and solitude, I recommend going early in the morning or late in the evening, when the crowds are thinner and the light casts a warm, golden glow over the landscape.

Finally, scheduling time to simply relax and unwind along the Régua riverfront is essential during your Douro River cruise. In these moments of quiet reflection, the true essence of the Douro Valley frequently emerges, leaving you with a profound sense of rejuvenation and a deeper appreciation for the captivating beauty that defines this remarkable region.

CHAPTER 7.

EXPERIENCING PINHÃO

Vineyard Touring and Wine Tasting

As the gentle waters of the Douro River carry you into the picturesque town of Pinhão, your eyes will immediately be drawn upwards, towards the undulating, terraced vineyards that cascade down the surrounding hillsides. This is the heart of Portugal's premier wine-producing region, and the opportunity to immerse yourself in the Douro Valley's captivating viticulture heritage is a must-do during your time in this captivating destination.

Pinhão farmyard near in Duor Valley

Take a guided tour of a family-owned Quinta, or estate, and experience firsthand the centuries-old traditions and meticulous craftsmanship that have defined this UNESCO-protected landscape. From the meticulous pruning and harvesting of the vines to the intricate blending and ageing processes that give each vintage its distinct character, these expertly curated excursions provide an unparalleled, behind-the-scenes look into the art of Douro winemaking.

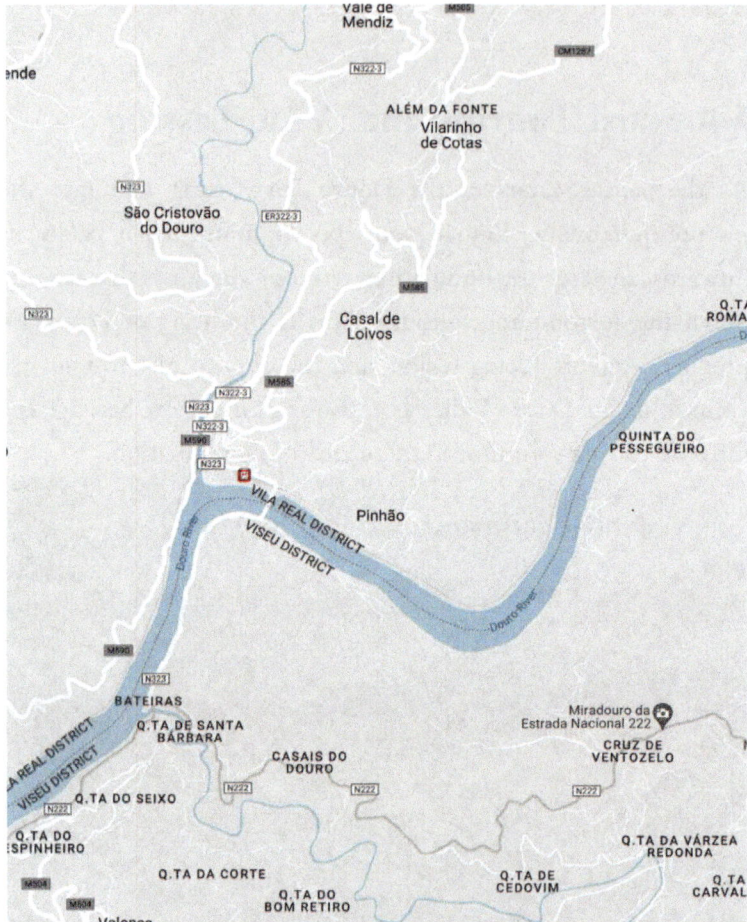

Engage with the knowledgeable guides and estate owners as they share fascinating insights and anecdotes, piqueing your interest in the region's distinct microclimates, traditional grape varietals, and innovative techniques that push the limits of what's possible. Their enthusiasm and pride are truly contagious, leaving you with a deep appreciation for the effort that goes into producing the Douro's world-class wines.

A visit to a Douro Valley vineyard is incomplete without a tasting, and Pinhão offers world-class options. Whether you choose to taste a variety of the estate's offerings, from bold, ruby-hued ports to luscious, amber-colored tawnies, or delve into the nuances of a single exceptional vintage, your palate will be delighted and enlightened.

Despite the abundance of well-known Quintas and vineyards in Pinhão, it's important not to become overwhelmed. To fully enjoy your wine-tasting experience, I recommend doing some research ahead of time, focusing on estates with the most compelling histories, engaging tour guides, and the best reputations for quality. This advance planning will allow you to fully immerse yourself in the enthralling world of Douro viticulture.

For those looking for a more immersive experience, many of the region's vineyards allow you to participate in the annual grape harvest or create your own personalised port wine. These hands-on activities not only make for unforgettable memories, but they also provide a visceral understanding of the Douro's winemaking traditions.

One final piece of advice: limit your alcohol consumption, especially if you intend to participate in multiple tastings or more strenuous activities such as hiking through the vineyards. Pace yourself, stay hydrated, and don't be afraid to spit out the wines you've tried; the goal is to enjoy the experience, not get drunk.

Responsible enjoyment is essential for ensuring that your vineyard adventures are both memorable and safe.

Exploring Douro Valley viticulture is a must-do during a visit to Pinhão. It provides an opportunity to enjoy world-class wines while also learning about the region's rich history, traditions, and artistry. With an adventurous spirit and an open palate, your explorations of the Douro's vineyards will undoubtedly be the highlight of your river cruise experience.

Scenic Train Ride Through the Valley

A beautiful train ride through this UNESCO-protected landscape is something I would strongly suggest adding to your itinerary as you immerse yourself in the fascinating town of Pinhão and the surrounding Douro Valley. This enthralling journey is sure to be the highlight of your time in the Douro, offering a singular and breathtaking perspective on the region's renowned viticulture and breathtaking natural beauty.

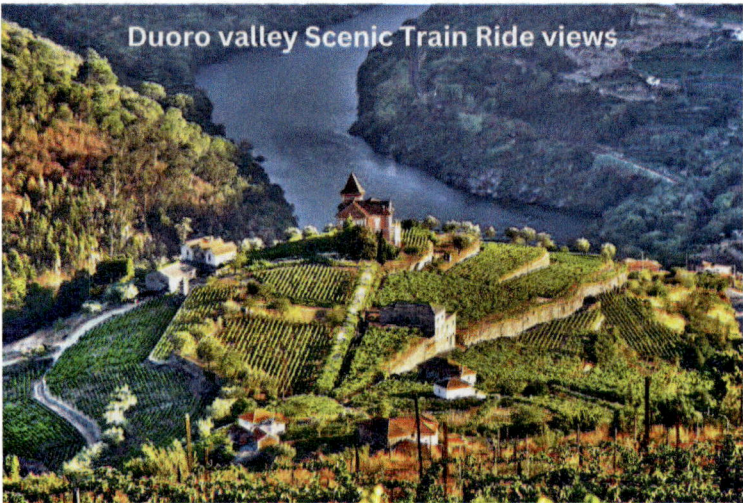
Duoro valley Scenic Train Ride views

Departing from the charming Pinhão train station, the journey winds its way through the undulating, terraced vineyards that have become the very emblem of the Douro Valley. As the train slowly chugs along, you'll be treated to an ever-shifting panorama of verdant slopes, punctuated by the telltale geometric patterns of the region's iconic vine-covered terraces. This is the heartland of Portugal's premier wine-producing region, and the opportunity to witness this captivating scenery unfold before your eyes is truly spellbinding.

One of the most enjoyable aspects of the Douro Valley train ride is the opportunity to fully immerse yourself in the region's rhythm and pace as the train navigates the serpentine curves and narrow passages that define this rugged, yet breathtakingly beautiful, landscape. Lean back in your seat, look out the window, and let the train's gentle sway transport you to a realm where time appears to slow to a more languid, contemplative tempo - it's in these moments that the true essence of the Douro often emerges.

As the train travels deeper into the valley, you'll be treated to ever-changing views that highlight the remarkable diversity of the Douro's natural wonders. View ancient quintas (wine estates) perched precariously on the hillsides, with vineyards cascading down to the river's edge. Admire the rugged, craggy ridges that rise majestically in the distance, bearing witness to the region's geological history. Keep an eye out for the traditional rabelo boats, the iconic flat-bottomed vessels that have long been used to transport the Douro's valuable port wine down the river.

I would encourage you to fully immerse yourself in the journey, stopping at each station to explore the charming villages and historic landmarks that line the train route. Each stop provides a unique opportunity to delve deeper into the Douro's rich cultural tapestry, whether it's strolling through the picturesque streets of Régua, admiring the Baroque grandeur of the Mateus Palace, or simply sipping a glass of the region's celebrated vinho verde at a local cafe.

One word of caution: as the Douro Valley train has grown in popularity, the carriages can become quite crowded, especially during peak tourist season. To ensure that you have the opportunity to fully enjoy the experience, I recommend purchasing your tickets in advance and, if possible, choosing an earlier or later departure time when crowds are typically thinner.

A scenic train ride through the Douro Valley is a must-do experience in Pinhão, providing a unique and captivating perspective on one of the world's most renowned wine-producing regions. Whether you're a nature lover, a history buff, or simply looking for a truly immersive and enchanting journey, this enchanting rail adventure will leave a lasting impression on your Douro River cruise experience.

Traditional Quintas and Wine Estates

The enchanting town of Pinhão and the breathtaking Douro Valley that surrounds it beckon with the promise of a truly immersive encounter – one that delves beyond the well-trodden tourist paths and into the very heart of this UNESCO-protected viticultural paradise. At the center of this captivating realm lie the centuries-old network of traditional quintas, or family-owned wine estates, each one a living, breathing testament to the Douro's rich winemaking heritage.

Heed the call of these historic properties, as they provide visitors with a unique opportunity to walk in the shoes of local winemaking families, experiencing firsthand the genuine passion and time-honored traditions that have defined this remarkable terroir for generations. Set aside any preconceived notions about stuffy, formal winery tours and instead embrace the warm hospitality and genuine connections that pervade these enchanting quintas.

Quinta do Seixo is a stunning property that has been in the same family for generations. As you walk through the meticulously maintained vineyards, tracing the contours of the terraced slopes, you'll be captivated by the estate owner's stories about the Douro's unique microclimate and the ancient winemaking techniques that have been lovingly preserved and passed down through the years.

The allure of these traditional quintas extends far beyond the vineyards and cellars, as the properties' architectural beauty is often spellbinding. Many feature grand, centuries-old manor houses with intricate tilework and decorative flourishes that reflect the region's Baroque heritage. Stepping into these historic spaces is like traveling back in time, immersing yourself in the opulence and elegance of a bygone era.

Of course, no visit to a Douro Valley quinta is complete without sampling the estate's renowned vintages, and the tasting experiences available at these properties are truly exceptional. Whether you choose a guided tour of the region's iconic port wines and crisp, refreshing vinho verdes, or you want to delve into the nuances of a single exceptional vintage, your palate will be captivated, and your appreciation for the Douro's winemaking prowess will be elevated to new levels.

However, as these traditional quintas have grown in popularity, it is critical to carefully plan your visits to ensure an intimate, immersive experience. Avoid the crowds by contacting the estates ahead of time and inquiring about private tours, tastings, or even the opportunity to participate in the annual grape harvest - these unique experiences will not only provide you with memories to cherish, but also a deeper connection to the Douro's rich cultural tapestry.

Exploring the traditional quintas and wine estates of the Douro Valley is a must-do during your stay in Pinhão, as it offers a chance to step beyond surface-level tourism and connect with the soul of this remarkable region. Accept the warm hospitality of the local winemaking families, and let their passion and time-honored traditions transport you to a realm where the true essence of the Douro emerges, one sip and story at a time.

CHAPTER 8.

CROSSING INTO SALAMANCA, SPAIN

Iconic Plaza Mayor

As your Douro River cruise carries you across the border into the captivating city of Salamanca, Spain, one of the true highlights that awaits you is the opportunity to immerse yourself in the grandeur and vibrant energy of the city's iconic Plaza Mayor. Often hailed as one of the most beautiful and well-preserved public squares in all of Europe, this magnificent Baroque masterpiece is a must-visit destination that will leave an indelible mark on your Iberian adventure.

City of Salamanca, Spain

Plaza Mayor

Upon first laying eyes on the Plaza Mayor, you'll be immediately struck by the sheer architectural splendour that defines this enchanting space. Flanked by a harmonious ensemble of golden-hued sandstone buildings, the square exudes an air of timeless elegance, with the ornate facades adorned in intricate carvings, arches, and balconies that speak to the region's rich cultural heritage. The centrepiece, of course, is the grand, two-tiered arcade that wraps around the perimeter, providing a covered walkway that invites you to stroll and soak in the lively atmosphere at a leisurely pace.

It is highly recommended that you spend some time strolling around the plaza and letting your eyes wander up to the fascinating spires and towers that pierce the sky above. The striking harmony and symmetry of the Plaza Mayor are incredibly alluring, and it's simple to get lost in the setting's overwhelming grandeur. Make sure you also look for the famous statue of King

Philip III, which dominates the center of the square and watches over the flurry of activity that goes on all around it.

However, the Plaza Mayor is more than just a visual treat; it serves as the hub of Salamanca's thriving cultural scene. There is always something going on in the square during the day, from live music and street performers to artisan markets, outdoor cafes, and lively social events. I would suggest that you fully immerse yourself in this enthralling ambiance by snagging a comfortable seat at one of the plaza's quaint cafes and enjoying a delicious tapas spread or a refreshing glass of local wine, all while taking in the sights and sounds that characterize this exceptional public space.

A word of warning, though: the Plaza Mayor can get very crowded, especially on weekends and during the busiest travel seasons, as it has grown in popularity among locals and visitors alike. I would suggest going either early in the morning or later in the evening, when the crowds are usually thinner and the light casts a warm, golden glow over the historic buildings, to make sure you have the chance to fully appreciate the grandeur and tranquillity of the setting.

In the end, a trip to Salamanca's Plaza Mayor is a must-do during your Douro River cruise because it provides an enthralling fusion of historically significant architecture, vibrant culture, and architectural grandeur that is simply unmatched. This famous square is guaranteed to make a lasting impression on your Iberian journey, regardless of your interests in history, architecture, or just finding a really engaging and magical public area.

Salamanca Cathedral

Towering majestically over the historic city of Salamanca, the twin spires of the Salamanca Cathedral stand as a testament to the region's enduring architectural and religious heritage. This awe-inspiring structure, which seamlessly blends the ornate Baroque style with the timeless elegance of Gothic design, is not only a UNESCO World Heritage Site but also a must-visit destination for any traveller seeking to delve into the captivating history and cultural riches of this enchanting Spanish city.

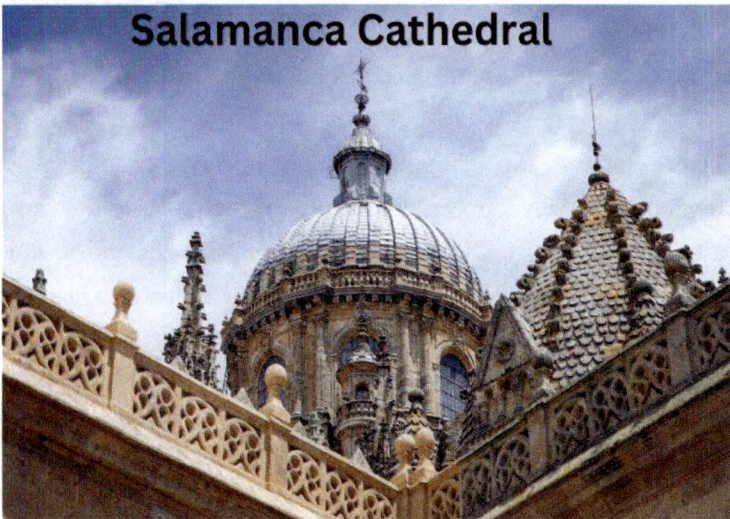

Salamanca Cathedral

As you approach the cathedral, the sheer scale and grandeur of the structure will immediately catch your eye, with intricate facades adorned with a dazzling array of sculptural details and ornamental flourishes that speak to the skill and artistry of the master builders who brought this remarkable structure to life centuries ago. The main entrance, also known as the "Plateresque" façade, is a true masterpiece of the Spanish Renaissance, with ornate carvings and decorative elements creating a mesmerizing visual spectacle that sets the stage for the spiritual and architectural wonders that await within.

Step through the cathedral's towering wooden doors and prepare to be completely captivated by its stunning interior. The vast, vaulted nave spreads out before you, its soaring arches and delicate, ribbed ceilings instilling a profound sense of reverence and awe. Looking up, you'll be treated to a spellbinding display of stained-glass windows that bathe the space in a kaleidoscope of jewel-toned hues, casting a warm, ethereal glow over the intricate stone carvings and ornate altarpieces that adorn the wall.

As you explore the various chapels and side aisles that radiate out from the central nave, keep an eye out for the cathedral's most iconic feature: the "Salmantina" chapel, a true gem of Baroque artistry with a breathtaking, gilded altarpiece that is simply awe-inspiring in its scale and opulence. The level of detail and craftsmanship on display demonstrates the artists' skill and dedication, and it's easy to become engrossed in the captivating interplay of light, shadow, and ornate decoration.

I would also recommend that you look for the cathedral's famous "hidden" figure, a playful salamander carved into the façade that has become a beloved symbol of Salamanca and a fun scavenger hunt for tourists. The search for this diminutive, elusive creature is an excellent way to engage with the cathedral's rich history and culture, and it will undoubtedly leave you with a greater appreciation for the meticulous care and attention to detail that distinguishes this extraordinary architectural gem.

However, as one of Salamanca's most popular attractions, the cathedral can get very crowded, especially during peak tourist seasons. To fully immerse yourself in the space and appreciate its tranquil, reverent atmosphere, I recommend going early in the morning or late in the afternoon, when the crowds are thinner and the light filtering through the stained-glass windows is most magical.

Finally, a visit to the Salamanca Cathedral is essential during your stay in this captivating Spanish city, as it provides a profound and lasting connection to the region's rich cultural and religious heritage. Whether you're an architecture enthusiast, a history buff, or simply looking for a truly awe-inspiring spiritual experience, this remarkable structure will leave an indelible impression on your Iberian adventure.

University of Salamanca

As you wander the enchanting streets of Salamanca, your eyes will inevitably be drawn towards the imposing, honey-hued edifice that dominates the city's historic skyline – the iconic University of Salamanca. Founded in 1218, this renowned institution of higher learning stands as one of the oldest universities in the world, and a visit to its hallowed halls offers a captivating glimpse into the rich intellectual and cultural heritage that has shaped not only Salamanca, but the very course of Western civilization.

Stepping through the grand, ornate gateway that serves as the university's main entrance transports you back in time, surrounded by the timeless beauty and architectural grandeur that has defined this remarkable institution for more than 800 years. The university's main building, known as the "Escuelas Mayores," is a true masterpiece of Spanish Plateresque style, with an elaborately carved façade and ornate towers that demonstrate the skill and artistry of the Renaissance-era craftsmen who created it.

As you wander the university's sun-dappled courtyards and cloistered passageways, keep an eye out for the numerous historical and architectural treasures that dot the campus, from the exquisite Baroque-style library to the captivating astronomical observatory that has played a pivotal role in the advancement of scientific knowledge. Every nook and cranny of this remarkable institution appears to hold a story waiting to be discovered, and the opportunity to delve into this rich tapestry of history is unquestionably the highlight of any visit to Salamanca.

But the University of Salamanca is more than just a showcase of architectural splendour; it is also a living, breathing center of academic excellence, with a long history of producing some of the world's most influential thinkers, scholars, and luminaries. I highly recommend taking one of the university's guided tours, which will not only provide you with a better understanding of the institution's history and significance, but will also give you a glimpse into the vibrant intellectual and cultural life that continues to thrive within its hallowed halls.

During your visit, make time to explore the university's renowned library, which houses rare books, manuscripts, and other priceless artifacts that provide a glimpse into the evolution of human knowledge and scholarship. The Library's stunning Plateresque façade, combined with the sheer volume of its collection, make it a must-see for any bibliophile or historian.

However, as the University of Salamanca has grown in popularity among visitors, the campus can become quite crowded, especially during peak tourist seasons and academic terms. To fully immerse yourself in the tranquil atmosphere and explore the university's many hidden gems, I recommend going early in the morning or late in the afternoon, when the crowds are usually smaller and the light casts a warm, golden glow over the timeless architecture.

Finally, a visit to the University of Salamanca is essential during your stay in this enthralling Spanish city, as it provides an opportunity to connect with the very source of Western intellectual and cultural thought. Whether you're a history buff, an architecture enthusiast, or simply looking for a truly enriching and enlightening experience, this venerable institution will leave an indelible mark on your Iberian journey.

CHAPTER 9.

ACCOMMODATIONS ALONG DOURO RIVER.

Top Rated Hotels and Inns

As you plan your captivating journey along the Douro River, the selection of your accommodations can greatly enhance your overall experience. From charming riverside inns to luxurious, full-service hotels, the Douro Valley offers a wealth of exceptional options to suit every traveller's needs and preferences. Let's explore some of the top-rated places to rest your head during your Douro River cruise adventure.

The Vintage House Hotel

Located in the heart of the picturesque town of Pinhão, the Vintage House Hotel is a true gem along the Douro River. This elegant, 19th-century manor house has been meticulously restored, blending its historic grandeur with modern amenities and impeccable service. Boasting panoramic views of the river and the surrounding vineyards, the Vintage House Hotel provides an authentic, immersive experience that captures the essence of the Douro Valley.

Guests can enjoy a range of amenities, including an outdoor pool, a revitalizing spa, and a gourmet restaurant serving locally-sourced, seasonal cuisine. With its prime riverside location and commitment to exceptional hospitality, the Vintage House Hotel is an ideal choice for those seeking a luxurious, yet quintessentially Portuguese, riverside retreat. Rates start at £250 per night. For more information and reservations, please visit their website at www.thevintagehousehotel.com.

Quinta da Pacheca

Nestled among the undulating vineyards of the Douro Valley, Quinta da Pacheca is a stunning wine estate that also provides a variety of charming accommodations. This historic quinta, or wine estate, has been meticulously restored, seamlessly blending centuries of history with modern comforts and amenities. Guests can choose from a variety of lodging options, including elegant rooms and suites in the main manor house, as well as private cottages and villas for a more secluded and tranquil experience.

Aside from the luxurious accommodations, Quinta da Pacheca has its own acclaimed winery, where visitors can participate in tastings, tours, and even hands-on winemaking experiences. Quinta da Pacheca, with its picturesque setting, rich history, and exceptional hospitality, provides a truly immersive and unforgettable Douro Valley experience. The rates start at £200 per night. To book your stay, go to www.quintadapacheca.com.

The Douro Royal Valley Hotel & Spa

The Douro Royal Valley Hotel & Spa, located on the banks of the Douro River, is a contemporary five-star oasis that provides unparalleled luxury and breathtaking views. This impressive hotel was designed with the discerning traveler in mind, and it boasts spacious, elegantly appointed rooms and suites, many of which have private balconies or terraces that overlook the river and surrounding vineyards.

Guests can enjoy the hotel's world-class amenities, which include a rejuvenating spa, a cutting-edge fitness center, and a variety of dining options that highlight the region's famous cuisine. Perhaps the hotel's most valuable asset is its prime location, which allows guests to easily explore the charming towns, historic quintas, and breathtaking natural landscapes that define the Douro Valley. Whether you're looking for a romantic getaway or a luxurious base for your Douro River cruise, the Douro Royal Valley Hotel & Spa is an excellent option. Rates begin at £350 per night. For reservations and additional information, please go to www.douroroyal.com.

Casa da Calçada.

Casa da Calçada, located in the picturesque town of Amarante, is a beautifully restored 16th-century manor house that provides a truly authentic and immersive Douro Valley experience. This charming boutique hotel seamlessly blends historic grandeur with modern amenities, offering guests a one-of-a-kind and intimate escape. Each of the hotel's individually decorated rooms and suites offers breathtaking views of the Douro River and the surrounding landscape, and guests can take advantage of a variety of amenities such as an outdoor pool, a gourmet restaurant, and a cozy library.

Casa da Calçada's location also provides easy access to the region's renowned wineries, hiking trails, and cultural attractions, making it an excellent starting point for exploring the heart of the Douro Valley. Casa da Calçada is a true hidden gem along the Douro River, offering warm hospitality, impeccable attention to detail, and a captivating historic setting. Rates begin at £180 per night. To book your stay, go to www.casadacalcada.com.

The Yeatman

The Yeatman, perched atop a hill with views of the Douro River and Porto, is a true sanctuary of luxury and sophistication. This five-star hotel is a must-see for oenophiles and discerning travelers alike, with an impressive collection of over 25,000 Portuguese wines and a Michelin-starred restaurant celebrating the region's exceptional cuisine.

Guests can unwind in the hotel's cutting-edge spa, swim in the outdoor infinity pool, or simply relax on their private balcony while taking in the breathtaking panoramic views. The Yeatman is the epitome of Douro Valley luxury, offering unparalleled service, impeccable attention to detail, and a prime location overlooking the Douro River. The rates start at £400 per night. To book your stay, go to www.the-yeatman-hotel.com.

Quinta Nova Nossa Senhora do Carmo

Quinta Nova Nossa Senhora do Carmo is a hidden gem for those looking for an immersive and authentic Douro Valley experience. This historic wine estate, nestled among the rolling vineyards, features a variety of beautifully appointed guest rooms and suites, each with its own distinct personality and charm. Guests can partake in the estate's well-known wine tasting experiences, hike the scenic trails, or simply relax and enjoy the peaceful, bucolic setting.

The on-site restaurant highlights the region's exceptional produce and culinary traditions, while the outdoor pool and terrace provide ideal places to relax and take in the breathtaking views. Quinta Nova Nossa Senhora do Carmo, with its commitment to sustainability, rich history, and exceptional hospitality, is a true haven for those looking to immerse themselves in the Douro Valley's authentic essence. The rates start at £200 per night. For more information and reservations, please go to www.quintanova.com.

These highly rated hotels and inns along the Douro River provide a wide range of accommodations, each with its own distinct charm and character. Whether you're looking for a luxurious, full-service resort, a historic wine estate, or a cozy, riverside retreat, the Douro Valley has something for everyone's tastes and budgets. By carefully considering your options and selecting the appropriate accommodations, you can guarantee a truly unforgettable and enriching Douro River cruise experience.

Unique Stays With River Views

In addition to the exceptional hotels and inns dotting the banks of the Douro River, the region also offers a wealth of unique accommodation options that provide an even more immersive and memorable experience. From cozy vineyard cottages to floating barges, these distinctive lodgings allow you to truly connect with the captivating essence of the Douro Valley.

Vineyard Cottages

These charming cottages, nestled among the Douro's rolling hills and terraced vineyards, provide a truly intimate and authentic retreat. Imagine waking up to sweeping views of the river and surrounding vineyards, as well as the opportunity to learn about the estate's winemaking operations through tastings and tours.

Many of these cottages have been lovingly restored, combining traditional Portuguese architecture with modern conveniences, and include private terraces, outdoor pools, and personal wine cellars. Staying in one of these vineyard cottages is essential for a truly immersive and tranquil Douro Valley experience.

Floating Barges

Consider staying on one of the Douro River's historic floating barges for a truly one-of-a-kind and unforgettable accommodation experience. These beautifully restored vessels, which were previously used to transport wine and other goods along the river, have been transformed into cozy, floating retreats. Guests can enjoy the gentle rocking of the waves, take in the ever-changing river views from the comfort of their own private cabin, and dine on-board using locally sourced ingredients. While the accommodations are small, the sense of adventure and the opportunity to immerse yourself in the Douro's rich nautical history more than compensate. Just make sure to book your barge experience well in advance, as they are in high demand.

Quintas with Guestrooms

The Douro Valley is home to numerous historic quintas, or wine estates, many of which provide a limited number of guest rooms or suites for visitors. These accommodations offer a truly immersive and authentic experience, with guests able to explore the estate's vineyards, tour the winemaking facilities, and enjoy private tastings and culinary experiences. Some of the more well-known quintas, such as Quinta do Crasto and Quinta da Pacheca, have beautifully restored guest rooms that seamlessly combine traditional architecture and modern amenities. By staying at a quinta, you'll not only enjoy stunning river views and peaceful surroundings, but you'll also gain a better understanding of the Douro Valley's rich wine culture and history.

Eco-lodges and Glamping Sites

For the more adventurous traveler, the Douro Valley has a variety of eco-lodges and glamping sites that offer a unique and sustainable way to experience the region's natural wonders. These accommodations, which are frequently located in remote areas or deep within the vineyards, allow you to immerse yourself in the breathtaking scenery while minimizing your environmental impact. Guests can choose from luxurious safari-style tents with plush furnishings to cozy, off-the-grid cabins with spectacular river views. Many of these eco-lodges also use sustainable practices like renewable energy and locally sourced, organic cuisine, adding to the authentic and responsible nature of your Douro Valley stay.

When considering these unique lodging options, keep in mind that they may require more advance planning and flexibility than traditional hotels. Availability can be limited, especially during peak season, and some may have specific check-in or transportation needs. However, the memories and experiences you'll have while staying at these one-of-a-kind Douro Valley retreats will be well worth the extra effort.

Budget-Friendly Options Along the Douro River

While the Douro Valley is renowned for its luxurious, high-end accommodations, there are also plenty of budget-friendly options that allow travellers to experience the region's captivating charm and beauty without breaking the bank. Whether you're seeking a cozy guesthouse, a charming riverside inn, or a conveniently located hostel, the Douro has something to suit every traveller's needs and preferences. Let's explore some of the top budget-friendly accommodations that the region has to offer.

Hotel Infante Sagres

The Hotel Infante Sagres, located in the heart of Porto and just a short distance from the Douro River, is a low-cost gem that provides excellent value. This historic hotel from the 1950s has been meticulously restored, combining mid-century modern design with modern comforts and amenities. Guests can expect well-appointed rooms with necessary modern amenities, as well as access to the hotel's cozy lounge, charming courtyard, and on-site restaurant, which serves delectable regional cuisine. While the Hotel Infante Sagres does not have the sweeping river views of some of the Douro's more luxurious properties, its prime location and affordable rates make it an excellent choice for those looking for a comfortable and conveniently located base from which to explore the city and the surrounding Douro Valley. Rates begin at £80 per night. For more information and reservations, please go to www.hotelinfantesagres.com.

Quinta de Lourosa

Nestled among the rolling vineyards and picturesque landscapes of the Douro Valley, Quinta de Lourosa provides a truly authentic and affordable accommodation option. This family-owned quinta, or wine estate, has been in operation for generations and now invites visitors to experience the region's rich heritage and hospitality firsthand. The property offers a variety of cozy, comfortable guest rooms as well as charming self-catering cottages ideal for those looking for a more independent and immersive experience.

Guests can explore the estate's vineyards, take part in wine tastings and tours, and eat locally sourced, homemade meals at the on-site restaurant. Quinta de Lourosa is an excellent choice for travelers looking to experience the essence of the Douro Valley at a reasonable price. Rates begin at £60 per night. For more information and reservations, please go to www.quintadelourosa.com.

Residencial Duorum

Residencial Duorum in Pinhão provides affordable accommodations with beautiful views of the Douro River. This family-run guesthouse has simple but comfortable rooms, all with private balconies or terraces that overlook the river and the surrounding vineyards. Each morning, guests can enjoy a delicious continental breakfast and have access to the property's cozy common areas, where they can relax and soak up the peaceful atmosphere. While the Residencial Duorum may not provide the same level of amenities as some of the Douro's more upscale hotels, its exceptional location, warm hospitality, and excellent value make it an ideal choice for travelers looking for a low-cost base from which to explore the region. Rates begin at £50 per night. For reservations and additional information, please go to www.residencialduorum.com.

Douro Hostel

For those looking for a more youthful and social accommodation experience, the Douro Hostel in Porto is an excellent low-cost option. Located just a stone's throw away from the Douro River, this modern hostel offers a variety of dorm-style and private room accommodations, all of which are designed with the traveler's comfort and convenience in mind. Guests have access to the hostel's shared kitchen and common areas, as well as organized activities and tours where they can meet other adventurers and immerse themselves in the city's vibrant culture. While the Douro Hostel does not offer the same level of privacy or luxury as some of the region's boutique hotels, it does provide an excellent value proposition and a fun, sociable atmosphere, making it ideal for solo travelers or groups on a budget. Dorm beds start at £20 per night, while private rooms cost £40. For more information and reservations, please go to www.douroriversidehostel.com.

Quinta do São Bernardo

Quinta de São Bernardo is a charming guest house nestled among vineyards and orchards in the Douro Valley, just a short drive from Porto's historic city center. This family-run establishment provides a variety of cozy, well-appointed guest rooms, as well as self-catering apartments and cottages that are ideal for those looking for a more independent and cost-effective stay. Guests can explore the estate's beautiful grounds, participate in wine tastings and tours, and eat homemade, locally sourced meals at the on-site restaurant. Quinta de São Bernardo offers a peaceful setting, warm hospitality, and great value for travelers looking to experience the authentic Douro Valley without breaking the bank. Rates begin at £70 per night. For more information and reservations, please go to www.quintadesaobernardo.com.

Casa do Barco

Consider spending a night or two aboard Casa do Barco, a historic barge that has been expertly converted into a cozy floating guesthouse. This one-of-a-kind lodging, situated along the Douro River, allows guests to immerse themselves in the region's rich nautical heritage while enjoying breathtaking river views and a peaceful, tranquil ambiance. The barge's compact but comfortable cabins are equipped with essential amenities, and guests can also use the shared lounge and outdoor deck areas. While the accommodations are smaller than a typical hotel room, the sense of adventure and the opportunity to sleep afloat on the Douro River make Casa do Barco a truly memorable and cost-effective choice. Rates begin at £60 per night. For reservations and additional information, please go to www.casadobarco.com.

Quinta da Boa Vista

Nestled among the rolling hills and terraced vineyards of the Douro Valley, Quinta da Boavista provides a charming and affordable guest house experience. This historic wine estate has been meticulously restored, and visitors can now experience the region's rich history and hospitality firsthand. The property has a variety of cozy, comfortable guest rooms, as well as a small number of self-catering cottages, all with stunning views of the surrounding vineyards and the Douro River.

Guests can explore the estate's winemaking facilities, participate in tastings and tours, and dine at the on-site restaurant, which serves locally sourced, homemade cuisine. Quinta da Boavista is an excellent choice for travelers looking for a low-cost, yet authentically immersive Douro Valley experience. Rates begin at £70 per night. For more information and reservations, please go to www.quintadaboavista.com.

Douro Valley Camping

The Douro Valley has a variety of scenic, eco-friendly campsites that offer a unique and affordable way to experience the region's stunning natural landscapes. These campsites, which are frequently located along the river's edge or tucked away in the heart of the vineyards, provide numerous opportunities for activities such as hiking, cycling, and even canoeing or kayaking.

Guests have a variety of accommodation options, including basic tent sites, cozy glamping setups, and even converted vintage caravans. Many campsites offer shared amenities like communal kitchens, hot showers, and recreation areas. While camping is not for everyone, it can be a very rewarding and cost-effective way to experience the natural beauty of the Douro Valley. Basic tent sites typically cost £20 per night. For more information and reservations, look into individual campsites or visit a camping resource website for the Douro region.

Whether you're looking for a charming guesthouse, a low-cost hostel, or the opportunity to camp under the stars, the Douro Valley has a variety of accommodations to suit every traveler's needs and preferences. By selecting one of these exceptional yet affordable options, you can experience the captivating essence of this remarkable region without breaking the bank, allowing you to concentrate on making unforgettable memories and discoveries along the Douro River.

CHAPTER 10.

BEST THINGS TO DO OR TRY IN YOUR DOURO RIVER CRUISE

Best Romantic Things to Try During Your Douro River Cruise

As you embark on your captivating journey along the Douro River, the region's enchanting landscapes and rich cultural tapestry provide the perfect backdrop for a truly romantic experience. Whether you're celebrating a special occasion or simply seeking to reconnect with your loved one, the Douro Valley offers a wealth of enchanting activities and experiences to make your cruise truly unforgettable.

Indulge in a Private Wine Tasting at a Historic Quinta

What could be more romantic than enjoying the Douro Valley's exquisite, world-renowned wines while surrounded by the region's breathtaking natural beauty? Many of the river's historic quintas, or wine estates, provide private tasting experiences, allowing you and your partner to explore the nuances of the Douro's celebrated vintages in an intimate, exclusive setting. Imagine sipping rich, velvety ports while gazing out at the undulating vineyards and gently flowing river - a truly idyllic and enchanting experience.

Embark on a Scenic Hot Air Balloon Ride

For a truly magical and unforgettable romantic adventure, book a hot air balloon ride over the Douro Valley. As you gently float above the region's patchwork of vineyards, olive groves, and winding river, you and your partner will be treated to breathtaking panoramic views. The peaceful, serene experience of drifting through the sky, accompanied only by the sound of the burners and the occasional call of local wildlife, creates a romantic and tranquil atmosphere.

Enjoy a Candlelit Dinner Aboard a Traditional Rabelo Boat

A delectable, candlelit dinner aboard a traditional rabelo boat will immerse you in the Douro River's rich nautical heritage. These iconic flat-bottomed vessels, which were once used to transport the region's celebrated ports and wines, now provide a one-of-a-kind and enchanting dining experience. As you float gently along the river, you and your loved one can enjoy a multi-course meal featuring locally sourced, seasonal ingredients and world-class Douro Valley wines, all while taking in the enchanting riverside scenery.

Unwind in a Private Riverside Spa Retreat

For the ultimate romantic pampering and relaxation, book a private spa experience at one of the Douro Valley's luxurious riverside retreats. Many of the region's top-rated hotels and quintas have serene, secluded spa facilities where you and your partner can enjoy soothing massages, rejuvenating facials, and other bespoke treatments while gazing out at the tranquil Douro River. This indulgent respite is the ideal way to unwind, reconnect, and make lasting memories from your Douro River cruise.

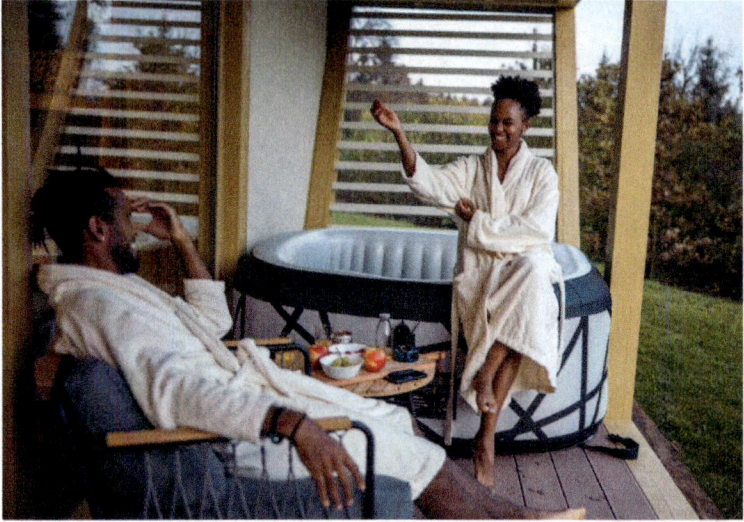

Explore the Douro Valley's Charming Villages Hand-in-Hand

Wander through the region's picturesque villages with your loved one to experience the authentic, unhurried pace of life along the Douro River. Discover local artisanal shops, sample delectable regional cuisine, and soak in the captivating ambiance of the Douro Valley in the charming settlements of Pinhão, with its iconic tile-decorated train station, and Peso da Régua's historic streets.

Embark on a Private Stargazing Cruise

As the sun sinks below the horizon, the Douro Valley transforms into a stunning canvas of twinkling stars and softly illuminated riverside views. Consider booking a private stargazing cruise, where you and your partner can bask in the peaceful beauty of the night sky, accompanied only by the gentle lapping of the river.

This enchanting excursion offers the ideal opportunity to reconnect, reflect, and create treasured memories to last a lifetime.

Whether you're planning a special anniversary celebration, a honeymoon, or simply a romantic getaway, the Douro River and its surrounding valley provide a plethora of enchanting experiences that are sure to rekindle passion and leave lasting memories. By embracing the region's natural splendour, rich cultural heritage, and world-class gastronomy, you and your loved one can create an unforgettable and romantic Douro River cruise experience.

Best Budget-Friendly Activities Along the Douro

While the Douro Valley is renowned for its luxurious accommodations and high-end dining experiences, there are also a wealth of budget-friendly activities and adventures that allow travellers to immerse themselves in the region's captivating essence without breaking the bank. From picturesque riverside strolls to enriching cultural experiences, the Douro has something to suit every traveller's interests and budget.

Take a Scenic Hike Through the Vineyards
One of the best ways to experience the Douro Valley's natural splendour is to lace up your hiking boots and explore the region's extensive network of scenic trails. Many of these paths wind through the area's iconic terraced vineyards, offering breathtaking vistas of the meandering river and the surrounding rolling hills. Best of all, these hikes are completely free to enjoy, allowing you to

immerse yourself in the beauty of the Douro without having to worry about the cost. Just be sure to pack plenty of water, snacks, and sun protection, and you'll be well on your way to an unforgettable budget-friendly adventure.

Discover Local History and Culture at Regional Museums

The Douro Valley is rich in history and cultural heritage, and many of the region's museums offer low-cost - or even free - admission, making them an excellent choice for budget-conscious visitors. The Museu do Douro, for example, in the charming town of Peso da Régua, offers an intriguing glimpse into the Douro's winemaking traditions as well as the lives of the people who have lived in this region for generations. Similarly, the Museu do Vinho in Lamego provides an in-depth look at the Douro's renowned wine industry, complete with interactive exhibits and tastings. By visiting these cultural institutions, you can gain a better understanding of the Douro Valley's past and present while staying within your travel budget.

Explore the charming streets of Pinhão.

Pinhão, also known as the "heart" of the Douro Valley's wine country, is a stunning and affordable destination. Wandering the town's charming riverside streets is a delightful, free activity that allows you to experience the Douro's authentic ambiance. Take in the iconic, tile-decorated train station, explore the local shops and artisanal workshops, and maybe even stop for a leisurely cup of coffee or a glass of the region's world-famous port wine. Pinhão's natural beauty and welcoming atmosphere make it a must-see destination for budget-conscious travelers.

Embark on a Self-Guided Cycling Adventure

For the more active and adventurous traveler, exploring the Douro Valley by bicycle is a great value. Many of the region's towns and villages are linked by well-maintained cycling paths and quiet country roads, allowing you to explore the area's breathtaking scenery at your leisure. You can bring your own bike or rent one locally, as many accommodations and tour operators provide convenient bicycle rentals. Just remember to bring a sturdy lock, a water bottle, and a map, and you'll be on your way to an unforgettable two-wheeled adventure down the Douro River.

Indulge in a Picnic by the River

One of the most inexpensive and enjoyable ways to experience the Douro Valley is to pack a picnic and find a scenic spot along the river to enjoy it in. Many of the region's parks and public spaces have plenty of green space and benches that overlook the water, making them ideal for a low-cost outdoor meal. Before your cruise, visit a local market or bakery to stock up on fresh, regional produce, artisanal breads, and possibly a bottle of the Douro's famous port wine. Then, find a peaceful spot to set up your picnic and take in the breathtaking natural beauty of your surroundings.

Attend a Free Local Festival or Cultural Event

Throughout the year, the Douro Valley hosts a variety of lively festivals and cultural events, many of which are free or very inexpensive for visitors. From the annual Douro Wine Festival, which honors the region's winemaking heritage, to traditional folk music and dance performances, these events offer an authentic, immersive glimpse into the Douro's vibrant local culture. By keeping an eye on event calendars and planning your trip accordingly, you can have a truly unforgettable cultural experience without breaking the bank.

Take a Scenic River Cruise on a Traditional Rabelo Boat

One of the most iconic and cost-effective ways to experience the Douro River is to take a cruise on a traditional Rabelo boat. These flat-bottomed vessels were once used to transport the region's famous port wines, but now they provide an affordable and authentic way for visitors to enjoy the valley's breathtaking riverside scenery. Many local tour operators provide short, inexpensive cruises that allow you to glide along the gentle waters and enjoy the picturesque scenery without breaking the bank. Just remember to dress warmly and bring your camera to capture the breathtaking views.

Explore the Charming Towns of Peso da Régua and Lamego

While the Douro Valley is known for its prestigious wine estates and luxurious accommodations, the region's charming towns and villages provide a plethora of low-cost attractions and activities. Peso da Régua and Lamego are two excellent places to visit. In Peso da Régua, you can stroll along the riverside promenade, admire the town's elegant 18th-century architecture, and even visit the Museu do Douro for a comprehensive look at the region's winemaking history. Meanwhile, the historic town of Lamego is home to a stunning Baroque cathedral, the impressive Sanctuary of Nossa Senhora dos Remédios, and a plethora of artisanal shops and local eateries, all of which are reasonably priced.

Immerse Yourself in the Douro Valley's Natural Beauty

For nature lovers, the Douro Valley provides numerous opportunities to immerse themselves in the region's stunning natural landscapes while staying within their budget. In addition to the hiking trails that wind through the vineyards, the region has a number of scenic parks and reserves that are free to visit. One such gem is the Parque Natural do Douro Internacional, a vast protected area with a diverse range of flora and fauna, as well as breathtaking views of the Douro River and the surrounding craggy cliffs. Simply lacing up your boots and setting out to discover the Douro's natural wonders will provide you with an enriching and cost-effective adventure.

By participating in these low-cost activities and adventures, you can fully immerse yourself in the captivating essence of the Douro

Valley while maintaining your overall travel experience. Whether you're hiking through the vineyards, visiting local museums, or simply enjoying a leisurely picnic by the river, the Douro offers a variety of enriching, low-cost options to suit every traveler's interests and preferences.

Best Family-Friendly Activities on the Douro

As a seasoned traveller along the Douro River, I can attest that this captivating region offers a wealth of engaging, family-friendly activities that are sure to delight visitors of all ages. Whether you're exploring the area's natural wonders, immersing yourselves in the local culture, or simply enjoying quality time together, the Douro Valley has something to capture the imagination and interests of both children and adults alike. Let me share with you some of my top recommendations for making the most of a family vacation on the Douro River.

Discover the Douro's Fascinating River Life at the Museu do Douro

One of the first stops I would suggest for families visiting the Douro Valley is the Museu do Douro, located in the charming town of Peso da Régua. This excellent museum offers an in-depth, interactive exploration of the river's rich history and the vital role it has played in the region's development. Children will be fascinated by the exhibits detailing the traditional methods of port wine production and transportation, complete with scale models of the iconic rabelo boats that once plied the Douro's waters. The museum also features hands-on displays that allow young visitors to learn about the river's diverse ecosystems and the local wildlife that call it home. With its engaging educational content and family-friendly atmosphere, the Museu do Douro is an ideal way to kick off your Douro River adventure and foster a deeper appreciation for this remarkable waterway.

Embark on a Scenic Train Journey Along the Douro Line

For a truly memorable family outing, I highly recommend taking the historic Douro Line railway, which winds its way along the river's picturesque banks. This vintage train journey provides breathtaking panoramic views of the Douro Valley's terraced vineyards, picturesque riverside towns, and dramatic rocky cliffs. Children will enjoy the train's carriages' old-world charm, and they will undoubtedly be astounded by the breathtaking natural scenery that unfolds before them. Keep an eye out for playful otters, majestic eagles, and other local wildlife, which can often be seen through the train's windows. This leisurely, family-friendly cruise is ideal for unwinding, relaxing, and taking in the allure of the Douro River.

Discover the Douro Valley's Enchanting Quintas and Vineyards

No trip to the Douro is complete without experiencing the region's world-renowned winemaking heritage firsthand. Many of the Douro's historic quintas, or wine estates, offer family-friendly tours and tastings, providing an intriguing glimpse into the centuries-old traditions of port and wine production. While the adults in your group will undoubtedly appreciate the opportunity to taste the Douro's celebrated vintages, children can often participate in enjoyable, educational activities such as grape stomping, learning about the bottling process, or exploring the estates' picturesque gardens and grounds. I especially recommend visiting Quinta da Aveleda, which has expansive, whimsically landscaped gardens that will delight young adventurers.

Soar Above the Douro Valley in a Hot Air Balloon

For a truly magical and unforgettable family experience, I recommend booking a hot air balloon ride over the picturesque Douro Valley. Imagine gently drifting above the region's patchwork of vineyards, olive groves, and meandering rivers, taking in the breathtaking panoramic views. This serene, peaceful adventure is an excellent way to introduce children to the Douro's breathtaking natural beauty, and the tranquil, weightless experience will leave an indelible impression on the entire family. Schedule your balloon ride for the early morning or late afternoon, when the light is most enchanting. And don't forget to bring your camera; the photo opportunities from above are simply breathtaking.

Explore the Douro's Aquatic Wonders with a Kayaking or Canoeing Adventure.

For families looking for a more active, hands-on way to explore the Douro River, I highly recommend going kayaking or canoeing. Many local outfitters provide guided tours that allow you to paddle along the river's calm, scenic waters, with the opportunity to see a variety of fascinating aquatic life, from playful otters to majestic birds of prey. Children will enjoy the thrill of powering their own vessel, while adults will appreciate the peaceful, meditative rhythm of paddling through the Douro's enchanting landscapes. These family-friendly water adventures provide an excellent opportunity to connect with the river's natural environment and make lasting memories together.

Immerse Yourselves in Local Cuisine and Culture at a Cooking Class

One of the best ways to truly immerse your family in the Douro Valley's rich cultural heritage is to take a hands-on cooking class. Many of the region's quintas and culinary institutions host family-friendly workshops where participants learn how to make authentic local dishes ranging from hearty stews to decadent desserts. Not only will children enjoy getting their hands dirty and learning new culinary skills, but the entire family will be able to bond over the shared experience of preparing a delicious meal together. Furthermore, you'll leave with valuable knowledge and recipes that you can replicate at home, allowing you to relive the flavors of the Douro long after your vacation has ended.

Discover the Douro's Enchanting Wildlife at Parque Natural do Douro Internacional

For families who enjoy nature and wildlife, I highly recommend visiting the Parque Natural do Douro Internacional, a vast protected area home to a diverse range of flora and fauna. This breathtaking natural reserve, which straddles the border between Portugal and Spain, provides numerous opportunities for hiking, birdwatching, and discovering the Douro's endemic wildlife. Children will be captivated by the opportunity to see charismatic creatures such as Iberian wolves, golden eagles, and Bonelli's eagles, all while immersed in the reserve's rugged, picturesque landscape. With well-marked trails and informative signage, the park is an excellent, low-cost option for families looking to experience the Douro's natural wonders.

Embark on a Picturesque Riverside Hike or Bike Ride

For families looking for a more active yet affordable way to explore the Douro Valley, I recommend going on a scenic hike or bicycle ride along the river's picturesque banks. Many of the region's towns and villages are connected by well-kept trails and quiet country roads, allowing you to explore the Douro's enchanting landscapes at your own pace. Children will enjoy the opportunity to burn off energy while surrounded by the area's breathtaking vineyards, olive groves, and dramatic cliffs. And for those who prefer a slower pace, the riverside promenades and pedestrian paths provide equally breathtaking views without requiring advanced fitness levels. Just remember to bring plenty of snacks, water, and sunscreen, and you'll be well on your way to an unforgettable family adventure.

Unleash Your Inner Pirate on a Rabelo Boat Cruise.

No trip to the Douro Valley is complete without experiencing the region's rich nautical heritage firsthand. For families, there's probably no more exciting way to do so than to go on a cruise aboard a traditional rabelo. These iconic, flat-bottomed vessels were once used to transport the Douro's famous ports and wines, but now they provide a fun, interactive way for both children and adults to learn about the river's fascinating history. As you float gently along the water, your children can imagine themselves as swashbuckling pirates, while the entire family enjoys the breathtaking riverside scenery. Many local tour operators provide family-friendly rabelo boat excursions, complete with engaging commentary and, in some cases, the opportunity to steer the vessel.

With so many engaging, family-friendly activities available, the Douro Valley is an ideal destination for both parents and children. By embracing the region's natural wonders, cultural heritage, and culinary delights, you and your loved ones can plan a truly unforgettable vacation full of discovery, adventure, and treasured memories. So pack your bags, gather the kids, and prepare to embark on an unforgettable journey along the captivating Douro River.

Uncovering the Douro's Hidden Gems and Off-the-Beaten-Path Delights

Based on my experience in travelling along the Douro River, I've had the pleasure of exploring not only the region's most celebrated sights and attractions, but also its hidden gems and off-the-beaten-path wonders. Thanks to the invaluable insights and recommendations from the friendly locals I've had the chance to meet and connect with along the way, I've uncovered a trove of enchanting experiences that truly capture the captivating essence of the Douro Valley. Allow me to share some of these extraordinary, lesser-known gems that I believe will elevate your river cruise to new heights of discovery and delight.

Discover the Enchanting Village of Favaios

Although Pinhão and Peso da Régua are well-known, Favaios is a hidden gem worth visiting. Favaios, located amidst the region's iconic vineyards, is well-known for its centuries-old tradition of baking the distinctive local bread known as folar. I highly recommend visiting the Padaria do Zé, a family-owned bakery where you can witness the time-honored process of making this delectable delicacy and possibly even try your hand at shaping the dough yourself. But the culinary delights don't stop there; Favaios also houses the Quinta do Convento, a historic wine estate that offers fascinating tours and tastings of its renowned Moscatel wines. Exploring this charming, off-the-beaten-path village provides a genuine, immersive glimpse into the Douro's rich cultural tapestry.

Go on a scenic hike through the Parque Natural do Douro Internacional.

While the Parque Natural do Douro Internacional is a well-known natural wonder along the Douro River, the park's extensive network of hiking trails provides ample opportunities for visitors to discover hidden gems and lesser-explored areas. Based on the advice of local nature enthusiasts, I recommend venturing beyond the main trailheads and immersing yourself in the park's rugged, untamed terrain. Keep an eye out for the elusive Iberian wolves, majestic golden eagles, and other endemic species that inhabit this protected area. Make time to explore the park's dramatic gorges, cascading waterfalls, and breathtaking vistas, which remain blissfully uncrowded. This immersive, off-the-beaten-path hiking adventure allows you to truly connect with the Douro's breathtaking natural beauty.

Indulge in a Private Port Tasting at a Family-Owned Quinta

While the Douro Valley's well-known wine estates are certainly worth a visit, I've discovered that some of the region's best port tastings can be found at smaller, family-owned quintas. Based on the enthusiastic recommendations of local wine experts, I would recommend scheduling a private tasting at a hidden gem such as Quinta do Beijo or Quinta de Sant'Ana. These intimate, off-the-beaten-path estates offer the opportunity to delve into the nuances of the Douro's celebrated port wines, guided by passionate, knowledgeable hosts who will share the unique stories and traditions of their family's winemaking legacy. This exclusive, behind-the-scenes look at Douro viticulture will leave a lasting impression.

Explore the Enchanting Streets of the Historic Town of Lamego

While the charming town of Peso da Régua frequently steals the spotlight along the Douro, I would strongly advise traveling a little further upstream to the lesser-known gem of Lamego. This historic settlement, with its winding cobblestone streets, elegant Baroque architecture, and stunning hilltop sanctuary, provides a captivating off-the-beaten-path experience in which you can immerse yourself in the Douro's rich cultural tapestry. According to locals, I would recommend wandering the town's picturesque streets, admiring the stunning Lamego Cathedral, and ascending the 686 steps of the Santuário de Nossa Senhora dos Remédios, a stunning 18th-century shrine with breathtaking panoramic views of the surrounding landscape. Exploring this enchanting, off-the-grid town will reveal a side of the Douro Valley that is blissfully untouched by tourist crowds.

Enjoy a Traditional Truffle Hunting Experience.
Participating in a traditional truffle hunting experience in the Douro Valley is a truly unique and immersive off-the-beaten-path adventure that I would strongly recommend. Based on the

enthusiastic recommendations of local chefs and foragers, I can confirm that this captivating activity provides an intriguing glimpse into a centuries-old regional tradition. Under the supervision of an experienced guide and their specially trained truffle-sniffing dog, you'll explore the Douro's oak and chestnut forests, learning how to identify and carefully harvest the elusive, edible fungi that thrive in the region's soil. After that, you'll be able to enjoy the fruits of your labor with a truffle-centric feast that will leave you with a renewed appreciation for this culinary treasure. This off-the-grid experience will undoubtedly be the highlight of your Douro River cruise.

Discover the Enchanting Charm of the Douro's Riverside Villages.

While the Douro Valley's more prominent towns like Pinhão and Peso da Régua deserve plenty of attention, I strongly encourage you to venture off the beaten path and explore some of the region's lesser-known riverside villages. Gems like Provesende, Ferradosa, and Barcos, for example, provide a peaceful, authentic glimpse into the Douro's rural heritage, complete with quaint, picturesque streets, traditional Portuguese architecture, and friendly locals. Based on the recommendations of the friendly residents I've met over the years, I recommend simply wandering these enchanting settlements, visiting local cafes and artisanal shops, and immersing yourself in the relaxed pace of life along the river. These off-the-grid experiences will leave you with treasured memories and a stronger connection to the Douro's cultural essence.

Indulge in a Unique Olive Oil Tasting Experience.

While the Douro Valley is well-known for its world-class wines, the region also has a thriving olive oil industry that is often overlooked. However, thanks to enthusiastic recommendations from local foodies and farmers, I've been able to discover some truly exceptional, off-the-beaten-path olive oil tasting experiences. I recommend visiting family-owned quintas such as Quinta de Marrocos or Quinta do Vallado, where you can learn about the Douro's centuries-old olive oil production traditions while sampling the region's best, most flavorful extra virgin olive oils. These intimate, artisanal tastings provide a unique and enriching perspective on the Douro's culinary heritage, and are sure to satisfy any discerning foodie.

Whether you're looking for hidden natural wonders, immersive cultural experiences, or exceptional culinary delights, the Douro Valley has extraordinary off-the-beaten-path gems that will take your river cruise to new levels of discovery and delight. By relying on the insights and recommendations of the friendly locals who call this captivating region home, you'll discover a treasure trove of enchanting experiences that will leave you with cherished memories and a deep connection to the Douro's essence. So set out on your journey with an adventurous spirit and an open mind, and allow the Douro's hidden treasures to reveal themselves to you.

CHAPTER 11.

TRAVEL TIPS AND INFORMATION

Budgeting and Managing Costs

One of the key considerations when planning your Douro River cruise is managing the costs associated with your journey. The good news is that there are numerous ways to ensure your trip remains within your desired budget, without sacrificing the quality of your experience.

First and foremost, I would recommend thoroughly researching and comparing cruise package options, as prices can vary widely depending on the amenities, excursions, and level of luxury included. Many cruise lines offer a range of cabin categories, from cozy staterooms to lavish suites, so be sure to weigh the trade-offs between cost and comfort to find the perfect fit for your needs and preferences.

For those looking to maximize their value, I recommend booking your cruise during shoulder seasons, when demand and prices are typically lower. The spring and fall months, for example, can provide significant savings over the peak summer season while still providing excellent weather and the opportunity to immerse yourself in the region's vibrant cultural events.

Another effective way to keep your costs under control is to carefully consider the optional shore excursions and activities available during your cruise. While these add-ons can improve your overall experience, they can quickly add up and deplete your budget. Review the itinerary carefully and choose only the excursions that are truly relevant to your interests and priorities, or look for opportunities to explore on your own for a more cost-effective option.

Consider the costs of dining, drinks, and other amenities when budgeting for on-board expenses. Many cruise lines offer all-inclusive or package pricing that can help you better manage your expenses, so look into those options. Furthermore, take advantage of any complimentary activities or entertainment offered by the cruise line, as these can help offset the cost of more elaborate shore-side excursions.

Finally, don't forget to budget for any additional travel expenses beyond the cruise, such as airfare, travel insurance, and any pre- or post-cruise hotel stays. By planning and budgeting for these additional expenses ahead of time, you can ensure that your overall trip stays within your desired budget.

Remember that the key to controlling your Douro River cruise costs is to strike a balance between maximizing your experience and avoiding unnecessary expenses. With some advance planning and a willingness to be flexible, you can create an unforgettable journey that fits perfectly with your budget and travel preferences.

The Ultimate Douro River Cruise Packing Guide

Packing for your Douro River cruise requires a thoughtful approach, as you'll need to strike a balance between keeping your luggage manageable while ensuring you have everything you need for a comfortable and enjoyable journey.

One of the most important considerations when packing for a river cruise is the limited storage space available in your cabin. Unlike ocean-going vessels, river cruise ships typically have smaller cabins, so it's essential to pack strategically and avoid bringing unnecessary items. I would recommend sticking to a single, moderately sized suitcase, as well as a smaller carry-on bag for any essentials you'll need during the day.

When it comes to clothing, opt for a versatile and functional wardrobe that can be easily mixed and matched. Comfortable, breathable fabrics that can be easily layered are ideal, as the weather in the Douro Valley can be quite unpredictable, with warm, sunny days and cool, breezy evenings. When exploring the region's charming towns and vineyards, bring a lightweight jacket or sweater as well as a sturdy pair of walking shoes or sandals.

Don't forget to bring any necessary toiletries, medications, and personal care items, as well as any chargers, adapters, or electronic devices you might need on your cruise. Consider bringing a reusable water bottle, a small backpack or day bag for shore excursions, and sun protection, such as a hat or sunglasses.

A small, collapsible umbrella or rain jacket is a must-have for your packing list. The Douro Valley experiences occasional showers, and having a reliable way to stay dry can make a big difference in your comfort and enjoyment.

Finally, try not to overpack. The less you bring, the more freedom and flexibility you'll have to fully enjoy your Douro River cruise experience. With a little planning and a focus on versatile, practical essentials, you can make sure you have everything you need without feeling weighed down by too much luggage. Anway, here is my full suggested ultimate packing list for this immersive journey through the heart of one of Portugal's most enchanting regions:

Carrier Bag

One of the most important aspects of your Douro River cruise packing strategy is the luggage solution you select. Investing in a high-quality, versatile carrier bag or suitcase can help you have a smooth and stress-free journey. Look for luggage that is both practical and stylish, with features such as four-wheeled design for ease of use, reinforced handles and lockable zippers for security, and water-resistant or waterproof materials to protect your belongings. A well-designed, compact yet spacious carrier can seamlessly transition from the airport to the ship, allowing you to focus on the exciting experiences ahead rather than the hassle of constantly repacking. By choosing the right luggage, you can set the stage for a truly carefree and enjoyable Douro River cruise adventure.

Luggage and Travel Essentials

The foundation of your Douro River cruise packing begins with a reliable and functional luggage solution. Look for a sturdy, yet lightweight suitcase or durable, versatile carry-on bag that can comfortably accommodate all your necessary items. Key features to consider include:

- Hard-sided or soft-sided construction for optimal protection
- Four-wheeled design for easy maneuverability
- Reinforced handles and lockable zippers for security
- Water-resistant or waterproof materials to safeguard your belongings
- Compact, collapsible design to maximize space

In addition to your main luggage, a small, comfortable backpack or day bag can be extremely useful for shore excursions and onboard activities, allowing you to keep essential items such as your camera, water bottle, and travel documents close at hand.

Clothing and Accessories

When packing for your Douro River cruise, prioritize versatile, comfortable, and weather-appropriate clothing that can be easily mixed and matched. The region's temperate, Mediterranean climate provides a variety of possibilities, so expect both sunny, warm days and the occasional cool or rainy spell.

Key items to consider include:

- Breathable, moisture-wicking tops and bottoms for daytime exploration
- Lightweight, packable outerwear like a rain jacket or windbreaker

- Comfortable, well-broken-in walking shoes or sneakers
- A few dressier outfits for special dining experiences or events on board
- Sun protection such as hats, sunglasses, and high-SPF sunscreen
- Swimwear and cover-ups if your ship has a pool or spa area

To ensure you have all your bases covered, it's also a good idea to pack a versatile, mix-and-match capsule wardrobe that can be easily adapted to the varying weather conditions and activities you may encounter throughout your Douro River cruise.

Toiletries and Personal Care

When it comes to personal care and toiletries, it's best to err on the side of caution and pack a comprehensive selection of items to ensure you're fully prepared. Some key considerations include:
- All necessary medications, both prescription and over-the-counter
- Travel-sized bottles of shampoo, conditioner, body wash, and other essential toiletries
- Makeup, skincare products, and any specialized hair care items you rely on
- Feminine hygiene products and a small nail care kit
- Earplugs and a sleep mask, if you tend to have trouble sleeping in unfamiliar environments

While some river cruise lines may provide basic toiletry amenities, it's always a good idea to have your own supplies on hand to maintain your personal care routine and ensure your comfort throughout the journey.

Electronics and Gadgets

In our increasingly digital world, it's essential to ensure your electronic devices are fully charged and ready to capture the stunning landscapes and memorable moments of your Douro River cruise. Some must-have items to pack include:

- Universal travel adapters and chargers for your smartphones, tablets, cameras, and other electronics
- Noise-cancelling headphones or earbuds for enjoying music, podcasts, or in-flight entertainment
- A portable power bank to keep your devices powered up, especially during shore excursions
- Your camera, extra batteries, and memory cards to document your journey
- An e-reader or tablet for reading, streaming, or gaming during downtime

Don't forget to also pack any necessary cables, cords, and protective cases to keep your electronics safe and accessible throughout your travels.

Miscellaneous Items

To round out your Douro River cruise packing list, consider the following additional items that can enhance your overall experience and provide a touch of convenience:

- Your passport, travel insurance information, and any other essential documents
- A small backpack or day bag for shore excursions and onboard activities

- A reusable water bottle to stay hydrated throughout the day
- A few of your favorite snacks or comfort foods
- A compact first-aid kit with bandages, antiseptic wipes, and pain relievers
- A travel pillow and blanket for cozy, restful journeys
- A small umbrella or rain cover to protect you from unexpected showers
- A dedicated travel wallet or document holder to keep your essentials organized

By thoughtfully curating this comprehensive packing list, you'll be well-equipped to embark on your Douro River cruise with confidence and ease, free to immerse yourself in the captivating sights, sounds, and flavors of this enchanting Portuguese region.

Travel Documentation and Identification

Ensuring that you have all the necessary travel documentation and identification in order is essential for a seamless and stress-free Douro River cruise experience. Here are a few key considerations to keep in mind:

First and foremost, make sure your passport is up-to-date and has at least six months of validity remaining. This is a mandatory requirement for travel to Spain and Portugal, and you won't be able to board your cruise without a valid passport.

Depending on your nationality and the duration of your stay, you may be required to obtain a visa in addition to your passport.

Make sure to look into the visa requirements for both Spain and Portugal well in advance of your trip, and apply for any necessary documentation well before your departure date.

If you intend to rent a car or participate in any other activities that require a driver's license, make sure to bring a valid, internationally recognized license with you. This will allow you to freely explore the region and take advantage of all available transportation options.

Make copies of your most important travel documents, such as your passport, visa, and any other identification cards. Keep these copies separate from the originals, either in a secure online storage system or in a different piece of luggage, so you have a backup in the event of loss or theft.

In addition, notify your bank and credit card companies of your upcoming travel plans to avoid problems with accessing funds or making purchases during your Douro River cruise. This will also help you prepare for any potential currency exchange or ATM usage during your stay in Spain and Portugal.

By ensuring that all of your travel documentation and identification are in order well before your departure, you can reduce the possibility of delays, hassles, or unexpected complications during your Douro River cruise adventure. A little forethought in this area can go a long way toward making your journey as smooth and stress-free as possible.

Travel Insurance Considerations

When planning a Douro River cruise, one of the most important steps you can take to protect your investment and your overall travel experience is to carefully consider your travel insurance options.

Travel insurance can be an important safeguard against a variety of potential problems, including unexpected medical emergencies, trip cancellations, lost or stolen luggage, and flight delays. By obtaining the appropriate coverage, you can have peace of mind knowing that you are covered in the event of any unforeseen circumstances that may arise during your journey.

When evaluating travel insurance policies, be sure to carefully review the coverage details to ensure that they align with your specific needs and concerns. Some key factors to consider include:

Medical coverage: Ensure that the policy provides comprehensive medical coverage, including emergency medical treatment, evacuation, and repatriation, as healthcare costs can be significantly higher in certain regions of Europe.

Trip cancellation and interruption: Look for a policy that provides comprehensive coverage for trip cancellations or interruptions caused by unforeseen circumstances such as illness, injury, or natural disasters.

Baggage and personal item protection: Consider coverage for lost, stolen, or damaged luggage and personal belongings, which can be expensive to replace, especially if you're traveling with valuables.

Travel delays and missed connections: Evaluate the policy's provisions for covering expenses incurred as a result of unexpected travel delays or missed connections, as these can have a significant impact on your overall trip experience.

Consider any pre-existing medical conditions or policy exclusions, as well as whether you need to purchase additional coverage for specific activities or destinations.

By thoroughly researching and comparing travel insurance options, you can tailor your coverage to your specific needs and budget, ensuring that you are fully protected throughout your Douro River cruise adventure. This investment can provide invaluable peace of mind and allow you to focus on making lasting memories without fear of unforeseen complications.

Getting Around the Douro Valley

Navigating the winding roads and charming towns of the Douro Valley can be a delightful and rewarding experience, but it's important to consider the best modes of transportation to ensure a seamless and stress-free journey.

One of the most convenient and picturesque ways to explore the region is by taking advantage of the Douro River cruise itself. These scenic waterborne journeys provide an intimate and immersive way to experience the valley's breathtaking landscapes, quaint villages, and iconic quintas (wine estates). I would highly recommend booking a cruise that offers a mix of on-board leisure and shore excursions, allowing you to fully immerse yourself in the local culture and history.

Renting a car can be a great option for those who want to be more self-sufficient. This allows you to explore the region at your own pace, taking in charming villages, hiking scenic trails, and visiting off-the-beaten-path wineries and attractions. However, I would warn that the roads in the Douro Valley can be narrow and winding, so use extra caution and patience when driving, especially in inclement weather or during peak tourist seasons.

Instead of driving yourself, consider taking a guided tour or hiring a private driver. These options are especially useful if you want to explore the region's famous wine country, as the drivers will be intimately familiar with the local roads and can provide valuable insights into the area's viticulture and history. Furthermore, these services can save you the hassle of parking and navigating unfamiliar territory.

Another enjoyable way to explore the Douro Valley is to take advantage of the area's extensive network of hiking and biking trails. These well-marked paths provide a unique perspective on the landscape, allowing you to enjoy the valley's natural beauty while also getting some light exercise. Just make sure to pack comfortable, sturdy shoes and plenty of water and snacks to keep you going on your adventures.

Regardless of your preferred mode of transportation, I recommend that you research and plan your routes ahead of time, taking into account road conditions, traffic patterns, and potential closures or detours. This will allow you to make the most of your time in the Douro Valley and ensure a smooth, trouble-free trip.

Remember that the key to navigating the Douro Valley is to strike a balance between independent exploration and guided experiences, while prioritizing your safety and comfort. With a little planning and a sense of adventure, you'll be able to make lasting memories as you explore the region's hidden gems and iconic landmarks.

Local Cuisine and Restaurants

One of the true highlights of any Douro River cruise is the opportunity to immerse yourself in the rich culinary traditions and world-class gastronomy that define this captivating region of Portugal. From the hearty, rustic flavors of traditional Douro Valley fare to the cutting-edge innovations of the area's renowned chefs, the local cuisine is a veritable feast for the senses that is not to be missed.

The iconic port wines that the Douro Valley is known for are central to the region's culinary landscape. These bold, complex elixirs are the ideal complement to the region's rich, flavorful cuisine, and delving into the nuances of these celebrated vintages is an essential component of any true culinary adventure. Whether you choose a classic pairing of port with a decadent chocolate dessert or you experiment with the versatility of these wines by sipping them alongside savory regional specialties, the Douro's food and drink are truly captivating.

Aside from the well-known port wines, the Douro Valley is home to a variety of other locally produced delicacies that are sure to please the palate. Artisanal cheeses, such as the creamy sheep's milk queijo da serra, are popular regional delicacies, while the area's famous cured meats, including the prized presunto (Iberian ham), pair well with the region's robust red wines. And no trip to the Douro is complete without indulging in the region's iconic bacalhau, or salted cod dishes, which have been a dietary staple for centuries.

Of course, the true heart and soul of the Douro's culinary landscape are its traditional, family-run restaurants, where generations-old recipes and time-honored cooking techniques combine to create dishes that are both deeply nourishing and profoundly evocative of the region's distinct cultural identity. These establishments, which are frequently tucked away in charming village squares or perched along the banks of the Douro River, provide an unparalleled opportunity to connect with the local way of life and immerse yourself in the distinct flavors that have been passed down through the generations.

Restaurante Rabelo in Pinhão is a must-visit for culinary enthusiasts. This family-owned restaurant, which has been a beloved fixture in the community for over 50 years, is well-known for its expert preparation of classic Douro Valley dishes, with each plate demonstrating the owner's unwavering commitment to using only the freshest, locally sourced ingredients.

When you walk into Restaurante Rabelo, you'll be struck by the warm, convivial atmosphere that pervades the space. The rustic-chic decor and panoramic views of the Douro River provide the perfect backdrop for an unforgettable dining experience. The menu is a veritable showcase of the region's culinary bounty, with standout dishes like the sizzling, garlic-infused carne de porco à alentejana (pork and clams), the rich and hearty arroz de forno (baked rice with meat and vegetables), and the impossibly flaky bacalhau à Gomes de Sá (salted cod with onions and potatoes).

However, the true star of **Restaurante Rabelo** is their renowned selection of port wines, which have been expertly curated to complement the robust, flavor-forward cuisine. The knowledgeable and attentive staff are delighted to guide you through the nuances of these celebrated vintages, providing insightful tasting notes and recommendations that will enhance your entire dining experience.

To ensure the best possible dining experience at Restaurante Rabelo, I strongly advise making reservations well in advance, as this popular establishment can quickly fill up, especially during peak tourist season. You can reach them at **+351 254 738 100** or via their website, www.restauranterabelo.com. Additionally, while the restaurant's dress code is casual and relaxed, I would recommend dressing smart-casual to fully embrace the convivial, sophisticated atmosphere.

However, Restaurante Rabelo is only the tip of the iceberg when it comes to the Douro Valley's culinary offerings. **Castas e Pratos,** located in the heart of Lamego's historic district, is another notable establishment that deserves your attention. This award-winning restaurant, led by renowned chef Rui Paula, has become a beacon of modern Portuguese cuisine, combining time-honored traditions with innovative, cutting-edge techniques to produce visually stunning and flavor-packed dishes.

When you walk into Castas e Pratos, you'll notice the restaurant's sleek, elegant design, which seamlessly blends rustic, natural elements with contemporary, minimalist flourishes. The dining room, with its sweeping views of the Douro River and the surrounding vineyards, sets the tone for an unforgettable culinary journey that highlights the best of the region's bounty.

The menu at Castas e Pratos is a true masterclass in dynamic, seasonal cuisine, with each dish demonstrating the chef's unwavering dedication to sourcing the freshest, locally grown ingredients and elevating them with his masterful touch. Standout dishes include the ethereal bacalhau com broa (salted cod with corn bread), the decadent posta mirandesa (grilled veal steak), and the mouthwatering arroz de pato (duck rice), all expertly paired with an extensive selection of the Douro's finest port wines and regional varietals.

Grilled veal steak)

However, the true highlight of a meal at Castas e Pratos is the opportunity to indulge in the restaurant's tasting menu, which provides a captivating, multi-course exploration of the chef's culinary genius. This immersive dining experience, which can be paired with a carefully curated selection of wine pairings, is a sensory feast that transports you through Douro's rich cultural and gastronomic heritage.

To secure your reservation at Castas e Pratos, I recommend contacting them well in advance, as this acclaimed restaurant is in high demand. You can reach them at **+351 254 613 263** or via their website, www.castasepratos.pt. Furthermore, while the dress code here is slightly more formal than at Restaurante Rabelo, I recommend wearing smart-casual attire to fully embrace the elegant, refined atmosphere.

In addition to the standout establishments of Restaurante Rabelo and Castas e Pratos, the Douro Valley is home to a plethora of other exceptional restaurants that deserve your culinary attention during your stay in this captivating region.

DOC, the Michelin-starred restaurant led by acclaimed Portuguese chef Rui Paula, is one such hidden gem that should not be missed. Located in the charming town of Folgosa, DOC provides an unparalleled dining experience that highlights the best of the Douro's abundant produce and world-renowned wines.

The serene, minimalist design of DOC will strike you from the moment you walk in, seamlessly blending rustic, natural elements with sleek, contemporary flourishes. The dining room, with its panoramic views of the Douro River and the surrounding vineyards, sets the tone for a truly transcendent culinary journey that is as much a feast for the eyes as it is for the taste buds.

The menu at DOC is a masterclass in seasonal, ingredient-driven cuisine, with each dish demonstrating the chef's unwavering dedication to highlighting the inherent beauty and complexity of the Douro's bounty. The ethereal bacalhau com broa e migas (salted cod with corn bread and sautéed greens), the decadent posta mirandesa com arroz de forno (grilled veal steak with baked rice), and the mouthwatering arroz de pato com enchidos (duck rice with cured sausages) are all expertly paired with the restaurant's extensive selection of the Douro's finest port wines and regional varietals.

However, the true highlight of a meal at DOC is the opportunity to indulge in the restaurant's tasting menu, which provides a captivating, multi-course exploration of the chef's culinary artistry. This immersive dining experience, which can be paired with a carefully curated selection of wine pairings, is a sensory feast that transports you through Douro's rich cultural and gastronomic heritage.

To secure your reservation at DOC, I would strongly advise you to contact them well in advance, as this acclaimed establishment is in high demand. You can reach them at **+351 254 489 020** or through their website, www.docrestaurante.com. While the dress code here is slightly more formal than at some of the region's more casual restaurants, I recommend wearing smart-casual attire to fully embrace the elegant, refined atmosphere.

Quinta da Pacheca, located in the heart of the Douro Valley's renowned wine country, is another exceptional restaurant worth including on your culinary itinerary. This stunning estate, which has its own acclaimed winery, provides a truly unique dining experience that seamlessly combines the region's rich viticultural heritage with innovative, contemporary cuisine.

As you approach the Quinta da Pacheca estate, you'll be struck by its breathtaking natural beauty, with rolling vineyards and stunning views of the Douro River serving as the ideal backdrop for an unforgettable meal. The restaurant, housed in a beautifully restored 18th-century manor house, exudes refined elegance, with a warm, inviting atmosphere and impeccable service that set the tone for a truly memorable dining experience.

Quinta da Pacheca's menu celebrates the Douro's bounty, with each dish demonstrating the restaurant's deep commitment to sourcing the best, locally grown ingredients and elevating them with the creative touch of the talented culinary team. Standout dishes include the rich and indulgent arroz de pato com queijo da serra (duck rice with mountain cheese), the delectable bacalhau à Gomes de Sá (salted cod with onions and potatoes), and the decadent baba de camelo (caramel custard), all of which complement the estate's award-winning port wines and regional varietals.

arroz de pato com queijo da serra

To make the most of your visit to Quinta da Pacheca, I recommend making a reservation in advance and taking advantage of the restaurant's tasting menu, which provides a multi-course exploration of the chef's culinary artistry. You can contact the restaurant at **+351 254 860 133** or visit their website at www.quintadapacheca.com. While the dress code is casual and relaxed, I recommend dressing smart-casual to fully embrace the refined yet welcoming atmosphere.

Aside from these exceptional establishments, the Douro Valley offers a plethora of other enticing dining options, ranging from the charming, family-run tascas (traditional taverns) that dot the region's quaint villages to the innovative, Michelin-starred restaurants that have put the Douro on the global culinary map. No matter where your culinary adventures take you, you can count on being treated to a sensory feast that celebrates the best of this captivating region's rich cultural and viticultural heritage.

Finally, the joy of experiencing local cuisine in the Douro Valley stems not only from the flavors themselves, but also from the opportunity to connect with the region's rich cultural heritage and the warm, welcoming people who have dedicated their lives to preserving and elevating these time-honored traditions. Whether you're savoring a perfectly prepared plate of bacalhau, sipping on a rare, vintage port, or simply enjoying the convivial atmosphere of a bustling local eatery, the Douro's culinary landscape will leave an indelible impression on your senses and heart.

When to Visit and Weather Considerations

When it comes to planning the perfect Douro River cruise, one of the most important factors to consider is the optimal time of year to visit this enchanting region of Portugal. The Douro Valley's temperate, Mediterranean climate offers a wealth of delightful possibilities throughout the seasons, each with its own unique charms and considerations.

For those looking to immerse themselves in the Douro's vibrant, sun-drenched splendor, the summer months of June through August are especially appealing. During the peak tourist season, the region is buzzing with activity, from the bustling markets and lively festivals that liven up the charming riverside towns to the verdant, rolling vineyards that appear to stretch on indefinitely under the warm, golden sunlight. The weather is usually sunny and dry at this time of year, with temperatures averaging a comfortable 25-30°C, making it an excellent time to explore the region's scenic hiking trails, attend wine tastings, and soak up the vibrant, convivial atmosphere.

However, it's worth noting that the summer months are also the busiest and most crowded times to visit the Douro Valley, with accommodations and transportation options frequently booking up well in advance. If you want a more peaceful, crowd-free experience, I recommend visiting during the shoulder seasons of spring (April-May) or autumn (September-October), when the weather is still mild and pleasant but the region is less crowded.

The spring season, in particular, provides a truly enchanting view of the Douro Valley, as the landscape transforms into a vibrant tapestry of blooming flowers and lush, green foliage. This is also an excellent time to see the region's renowned winemaking in action, as the vineyards come alive with the frenzy of the annual harvest. And, with summer crowds still to come, you'll be able to explore the area's charming towns and historic quintas (wine estates) at your leisure, immersing yourself in local culture and traditions.

In contrast, the autumn months of September and October offer a decidedly more serene, introspective view of the Douro Valley, as the landscape transforms into a breathtaking display of golden hues and the harvest season comes to an end. This is an excellent time to sample the region's renowned port wines, as the cellars and tasting rooms take on a cozy, convivial atmosphere, and the weather is mild and pleasant enough for outdoor exploration and dining.

Regardless of the season you choose, keep in mind the region's changing weather patterns and plan accordingly. While the Douro Valley has a Mediterranean climate with mild, sunny weather for most of the year, sudden temperature changes and the occasional rainstorm are not uncommon. I would strongly advise packing layers and bringing a dependable rain jacket or umbrella, as even the brightest days can be interrupted by brief, refreshing showers.

Furthermore, the Douro River itself may experience occasional disruptions, such as low water levels or closures, especially during the drier summer months. While cruise lines and tour operators work hard to address these issues, it's always a good idea to be aware of any potential changes or alterations to your itinerary.

Finally, the best time to visit the Douro Valley is the one that most closely matches your personal preferences and travel objectives. Whether you want to bask in the vibrant, sun-drenched splendor of summer, immerse yourself in the region's springtime bloom, or enjoy the tranquil, autumnal beauty of the Douro, there are plenty of captivating opportunities to discover the true magic of this enchanting Portuguese gem.

Useful Portuguese Phrases

As you embark on your journey through the enchanting Douro Valley, one of the most valuable tools in your travel arsenal will be a working knowledge of the local language – Portuguese. While many of the region's residents, particularly those working in the tourism industry, will have a good grasp of English, familiarizing yourself with at least a few key Portuguese phrases can greatly enhance your overall experience and help you forge a deeper connection with the local culture.

To get you started, here are some of the most useful Portuguese phrases to have in your repertoire:

Greetings and Introductions:
- Olá (oh-lah) – Hello
- Bom dia (boum dee-ah) – Good morning
- Boa tarde (boh-ah tar-deh) – Good afternoon
- Boa noite (boh-ah no-ee-teh) – Good evening
- Por favor (por fah-vor) – Please
- Obrigado/a (oh-bree-gah-doo/ah) – Thank you (masculine/feminine)
- Desculpe (deh-skool-peh) – Excuse me

Basic Conversational Phrases:

- Fala inglês? (fah-lah een-glesh) – Do you speak English?
- Não entendo (nown en-ten-doo) – I don't understand
- Pode repetir, por favor? (poh-deh reh-peh-teer, por fah-vor) – Could you please repeat that?
- Compreendo (kom-preh-en-doo) – I understand
- Eu não compreendo (eh-oo nown kom-preh-en-doo) – I don't understand
- Quanto custa? (kwan-toh koosh-tah) – How much does it cost?

- Onde fica...? (on-deh fee-kah) – Where is...?

Dining and Ordering:
- Eu gostaria de... (eh-oo gosh-tah-ree-ah deh) – I would like...
- Posso ver o menu, por favor? (poh-soo vair oo men-oo, por fah-vor) – May I see the menu, please?
- Eu vou querer... (eh-oo voh keh-rair) – I will have...
- A conta, por favor (ah kon-tah, por fah-vor) – The bill, please

Transportation:
- Onde fica a estação de comboios? (on-deh fee-kah ah eh-stah-sown deh komb-boy-ohs) – Where is the train station?
- Quanto custa o bilhete? (kwan-toh koosh-tah oo bee-yeh-teh) – How much is the ticket?
- Pode me indicar o caminho? (poh-deh meh een-dee-kar oo kah-meen-yoo) – Can you show me the way?
- Vire à esquerda/direita (vee-reh ah esh-ker-dah/dee-ray-tah) – Turn left/right

While these are just a few of the many Portuguese phrases you might find useful on your Douro Valley adventure, don't be afraid to experiment and interact with the locals. A genuine attempt to communicate in their native language, even with limited proficiency, will be greatly appreciated and can lead to meaningful connections and unforgettable experiences.

Remember, the people of the Douro Valley are known for their warm hospitality and genuine friendliness, so don't be afraid to put your Portuguese to the test. With some practice and a willingness to embrace the local culture, you'll be able to navigate the region like a true local in no time.

Best Money-Saving Tips for Your Douro River Cruise

Embarking on a Douro River cruise can be a truly transformative and unforgettable experience, but it's important to approach the planning and budgeting process with a strategic mindset to ensure that you get the most value for your money. With a few savvy money-saving tips and practices, you can maximize your enjoyment of this captivating region without breaking the bank.

One of the most effective ways to save money on your Douro River cruise is to book well in advance. Many cruise lines and tour operators provide substantial early booking discounts, sometimes up to a year or more before your planned departure date. Taking advantage of these promotions allows you to secure your spot on your preferred itinerary while saving a significant amount of money.

In addition to early booking discounts, look for other promotional offers and package deals that allow you to combine your cruise with airfare, hotel accommodations, or even pre- or post-cruise excursions. These bundled packages frequently represent a significant cost savings over booking each element separately, and they can provide a more seamless and cohesive travel experience.

Another important strategy for saving money on your Douro River cruise is to be flexible about your travel dates. Prices can vary significantly depending on the time of year and even the day of the week, so consider rescheduling your trip by a day or two to benefit from lower rates. Additionally, looking into shoulder season options (such as April-May or September-October) can result in significant savings while still providing pleasant weather and a less crowded experience.

When it comes to onboard expenses, one of the best ways to stay within your budget is to take advantage of the all-inclusive nature of many Douro River cruise packages. These packages typically include a variety of amenities, such as meals and beverages, shore excursions, and entertainment, all bundled into a single, predictable price. By choosing an all-inclusive package, you can avoid the temptation of unnecessary or unplanned spending and have a more carefree, hassle-free cruise vacation.

Consider bringing your own reusable water bottle and snacks to avoid having to buy these items onboard, where prices can be high. When it comes to shore excursions, look into any free or low-cost options that match your interests, such as self-guided walking tours or visits to local markets and vineyards.

Finally, don't be afraid to take advantage of any loyalty programs or credit card rewards that may be available for your Douro River cruise reservation. Many cruise lines and travel companies offer rewards programs that can result in significant savings, and certain credit cards may offer additional benefits or discounts on travel-related expenses.

By incorporating these money-saving tips and best practices into your Douro River cruise itinerary, you will be able to enjoy the full splendor of this captivating region without worrying about overspending. With some strategic budgeting and a willingness to consider alternative options, you can plan an unforgettable trip that perfectly aligns with your financial objectives.

Thanks for purchasing this book and reading up to the last page. If this book has been helpful to you, I am kindly requesting you to rate it and leave an honest review. Feel very much appreciated. I wish you safe travels.

Printed in Great Britain
by Amazon